Praise

Danny will educate and inspire you into a life of reading and personal growth.

—*Brian Tracy, Legendary Speaker & Bestselling Author*
The Power of Self-Confidence

Danny Brassell is an extremely dynamic speaker who is passionate about kids and literacy. If you haven't had the opportunity to hear him in person, this is the perfect (presentation) to get you excited about teaching.

—*Laura Numeroff, Author*
If You Give a Mouse Cookie

Today, despite my success, I am a slow reader, and thus a slow learner. This is why I love what Danny does. He teaches us how to instill a passion and a skill for reading in children, and he does it in a way that is both entertaining and compelling.

—*Lia Grimalis, voted one of*
Canada's 100 Most Powerful Women

Here's the thing about Danny. You come away not only inspired, but with dozens of practical innovations to add to your own teaching bag of tricks. The man is a cornucopia of ideas and suggestions.

—*Will Hobbs, Author*
Ghost Canoe

Danny Brassell was quite funny.

—*Sonia Marzano, Author & Actress*
"Maria" on Sesame Street

You asked for it! Danny's unique form of humor and speaking style has made him a schoolhouse word nationally. His straight-forward, commonsense advice (is great) for educators at every level.

—*Jim Grant, Executive Director*
Staff Development for Educators

After meeting Danny it is hard not to be excited about your goals. (His presentation) is a wonderful blend of tips and stories illustrating the importance of reading and how reading is an integral part of your success.
–*Terri Harden, Artist & Imagineer*
Walt Disney Company

Danny combines real-life experiences, humor and effective strategies to show how to have fun and still meet instructional goals. Danny helps educators remember what makes them happy, how to stay positive and why they make a difference for students.
–*Edward J. Albert, Superintendent*
Tulpehocken Area School District

Every educator, parent, policymaker and student needs to listen to Danny. His passion for literacy is unparalleled, and his energy and enthusiasm are sure to leave you mesmerized and eager to run to your local bookstore.
–*Sheri Fink, Author*
The Little Rose

I had the wonderful experience of hearing Dr. Brassell speak before a crowd of Beverly Hills business leaders, and he was not only able to hit his target message but he was successful in bringing back the child in all of us.
–*Bryan Monfort, Vice President of Operations*
Lawry's Restaurants

Danny is a cross between Jim Carrey and Robin Williams…If you don't walk away from his seminar with ideas you can use tomorrow, you were unconscious during the presentation.
–*Nancy Bebrin, ESL Teacher*
Quaker Farms School

Leadership in every sector can benefit from hearing Danny, as he dynamically and with humor provides so many examples of how leaders apply their perspectives and experiences in diverse environments. His skill in linking the lessons learned by children and the ability to apply those (lessons) in leadership roles is exceptional.
–*Lila Larson, Former National Leadership Development Consultant*
IBM Global Services – Canada

Danny is a polished speaker, but most importantly his heart shines through in his work. His genuine efforts to make a positive difference in people's lives is obvious. Danny is a class act, and I enthusiastically recommend his work!
–Pamela Haack, Founder
The Italy Retreat for Women Business Leaders and Entrepreneurs

If you are looking for a MAGICAL experience for your event, Danny Brassell is one of the most dynamic and amazing speakers you will ever hear…an incredible presentation and inspiring message. It is an absolute must for any leader or business team. Don't hesitate. Book him NOW!
–John Formica
America's Customer Experience Coach

Impactful! From the top business leader to the essential hourly employee, Dr. Danny Brassell unveils and easy, memorable pathway to achievement.
–Elizabeth McCormick
Former U.S. Army Blackhawk Pilot

Danny is a purely awesome unstoppable positive force of nature! We need more people like him in the world, and it makes me smile knowing that there are so many who get to learn from him.
–Wayne Logue, Creator
Wordtoons

Nothing could have been better for our teachers to start the year off on a positive note. Danny engaged and motivated all of our teachers from pre-K to high school, first year to 30-year vets, with stories from the classroom and life. His energy and passion for literacy generated a standing ovation and is something teachers still talk about.
–Robert Schwartz, Chief Academic Officer
ICEF Public Schools

Danny aspires to bring the best out of an individual by using his charismatic enthusiasm, humor and motivational skills. It was evident that our employees walked away inspired and were eager for more Danny.
–Daniela Sabo, Human Resources Coordinator
AEG-Staples Center and Nokia Theater L.A. Live

I was in awe of Danny. There were a few hundred people in the room…a great mixture of leaders in the fields of business, entertainment and education. I love the way he masterfully crafted his message in a way that left (attendees) with practical takeaways we could implement right away. I really loved the way he supported his much-needed message with credible and topical research. Not only did he motivate me, but Danny also gave me ideas and some solutions for my business that I never thought of.

–Kalani Vale, Former #1 Trainer
Tony Robbins (Robbins Research International, Inc.)

From start-up entrepreneurs to the world's most powerful CEOs, Danny can and will teach anyone how to be successful and much happier doing what they love to do.

–Kevin Knight, President
Liberty Management

The best advocate for literacy and the love of reading. With his extensive knowledge and real-world experience in the classroom, he wins over veteran educators (by living) the ideal that 'learning is fun.' Tutors walk out ready, equipped, and excited to share the love of reading with any child. His trainings were so popular that seasoned school teachers, counselors and librarians took the day off to participate. It was a privilege to work with him and especially to learn from him all these years.

–Tarry Kang, Volunteer Program Coordinator
The Wonder of Reading

(Danny) is very knowledgeable on professional issues, and he has a unique ability to engage and communicate with audiences of in-service and pre-service teachers, school administrators and parents.

–Tim Rasinski, Professor and Member of the
National Reading Hall of Fame
Kent State University

Let Danny be your coach, and he will show you that not all readers are leaders, but all leaders are readers. He will make you laugh, cry and think – sometimes within the same sentence.

–Jaymin J. Patel
Consultant & Fortune 500 Advisor

If you want to reignite the passion from your inner core and see the world through a validating and joyful lens, Dr. Brassell is your man. He's dynamic, relevant, passionate and practical! He shares tried and true methods that have worked throughout time to capture the hearts and minds of humanity. He is a living artist painting classrooms of community, love, learning and excellence. Thank you for elevating the greatest profession on earth!
–Rebecca Coda, NBCT, K-6 Director of Curriculum & Instruction
Cabot Public Schools

Danny is an amazing presenter! His talk and approach to creating a positive learning environment is applicable to all…He truly motivated my staff to make a difference.
–Erikk Aldridge, Executive Director
Boys & Girls Club of Venice

For those people who desire to move forward in life, to grow and to expand, Danny shows the power of how reading transforms a wish into an achievement. Danny has the strength of a storyteller who entertains while weaving an educational message throughout each talk. Invite Danny to coach you from your dreams to a new reality.
–Sherry M. Winn
NCAA National Championship Women's Basketball Coach

Danny Brassell is a top-notch leadership and business speaker. He takes leaders to the next level and beyond. His strategies inspire leaders to achieve extraordinary results! Above all, Danny is a man of integrity and a true example of a real leader.
–Matt Jones, Founder
R.E.A.L. Leadership Academy

I left feeling motivated, energized and renewed! Danny's practical passion is infectious and something that ALL educators must experience. I am confident that I can make a difference in the lives of the students.
–Melissa Baker, Title I Lead Extension Teacher
Bridge City Elementary School

If you need to hit a home run selecting a speaker, then you need to choose Dr. Danny Brassell. His unique perspective is not only engaging and entertaining but educates in a way that translates into high value for your audience. Your audience will love the creative, high-energy way his stories communicate an important message, leaving everyone wanting for more. Choose Danny, and your audience will be the benefactor of a truly memorable experience.
–*Richard L. Davis, CEO & President*
Arbor Scientia Group

"I felt very much engaged through Danny's entire presentation. It was entertaining, rewarding and educational."
–*Barouch Chai, President/CEO*
Microcomputer Science Centre Inc.

"Danny was one of our most entertaining and engaging speakers. Full of great information and enthusiasm. Parents and teachers loved his fast-paced presentation. We look forward to having (him) back again."
–*Kristina Jackson, Parent Talk Coordinator*
South Bay Adult School

"Students and parents left (Danny's) presentation so enthusiastic about reading that they are still talking about it. He is the only speaker we have ever had who received a standing ovation."
–*Edna Moore, Principal*
Palm Elementary School

"Danny's reading presentation should be required viewing in every school in the country. I am a first-year teacher in a small charter school with a passion for creating third graders who love to read. Now I have the tools to make that happen!"
–*Barry Kaiser, Third Grade Teacher*
Sonoran Science Academy

"Danny's enthusiasm was contagious and his personal experiences made the presentation informative and relevant. Some people may find it daunting to energize and motivate a large group of administrators after completing statewide testing, but Danny 'knocked our socks off.' We were ready for any challenge after listening to his inspiring presentation."
–*Robert L. Wagner, President*
Maryland Association of Elementary School Principals

SUCCESS BOOKS

THE READING BREAKTHROUGH

Affectionately known as "Jim Carrey with a Ph.D.," Dr. Danny Brassell (www.DannyBrassell.com) is an internationally-acclaimed speaker and best-selling author of 15 books, including *Read, Lead & Succeed* and *The Reading Makeover*, based on his popular TEDx talk. A gregarious, sought-after author, speaker and business consultant, Danny is a recognized authority on leadership development, reading, motivation and communication skills and the co-founder of the world's top reading engagement system, www.ReadBetterin67Steps.com, which shows parents how to help their struggling or reluctant readers turn into more passionate and proficient readers. His mission is to bring joy back into education and the workplace. Thousands, from school districts to businesses to association conferences, have enjoyed his energetic, interactive and informative presentations. He has spoken to over 2,500 different audiences worldwide.

AUTHOR'S NOTE

This book project initially commenced in 2006, based on my work as the volunteer trainer for a wonderful (now defunct) non-profit organization known as The Wonder of Reading, which literally created hundreds of libraries in under-resourced schools throughout the Greater Los Angeles area. I am indebted to that organization, its recipient schools and the thousands of volunteers I trained during that time. My experience taught me the value of supporting anyone interested in assisting struggling or reluctant readers and how little effort it took to produce significant results in students. The key – I learned – was providing teachers and parents with simple steps that did not require extensive time or background knowledge, on their part. Thus, this system is the precursor to the world's most successful reading engagement program, www.ReadBETTERin67Steps.com, that I co-founded with my business partner, Nestor Santtia. The ideas in this book greatly inform that program.

DANNY BRASSELL, Ph.D.
"America's Leading Reading Ambassador"

A few words of Motivation and Inspiration:

"Readers are not necessarily leaders, but I have NEVER met a leader who is not a voracious reader."

"When you go through life trying to be like everyone else, that's all you'll ever be – like everyone else."

"You are what you read, so read good stuff."

"The secret to success can be found on the shelves of libraries."

"Education is valuable, but execution is priceless."

The Ideal Professional Speaker for Your Next Event!

Schedule Danny to Speak at Your Event!
(310) 872-9089 • www.DannyBrassell.com

Success Press
A division of Go Habit Pro
No 10/1. 2nd Floor, 1st St.
Chowdry Nagar, Valasaravakkam
Chennai, Tamil Nadu 600087 India
www.GoHabitPro.com

Offices and agents throughout the world

© 2018 by Danny Brassell

All rights reserved. No part of this book may be reproduced in any form or by any electronic or mechanical means, including information storage and retrieval systems, without permission in writing from the publisher, except by a reviewer, who may quote brief passages in a review, with the exception of the reproducibles (identified by the THE READING BREAKTHROUGH copyright line), which may be photocopied for classroom use.

Library of Congress Cataloging-in-Publication Data
Brassell, Danny.
The Reading Breakthrough / Danny Brassell.
     p. cm.
Includes bibliographical references and index.

ISBN-13: 978-1724628473 (alk. paper)

1. Reading (Elementary).   2. Parenting.   3. Education.   I. Title.

Acquisitions editor: Nestor Santtia
Production: Sam Belmonte
Cover design: Janice Gerson
Typesetter: Alejo Diaz Bueno
Manufacturing: R.C. Simon
Distribution: Mo Smead

Printed in the United States of America on acid-free paper
10 09 08 07 06 VP 1 2 3 4 5

This book is dedicated to all those who work to ensure that reading is always a pleasure, never a chore.

CONTENTS

Foreword by Jim Trelease — xvii
Acknowledgments — xix
Preface — xxi
Introduction — xxiii
    The Author — xxv
    The Problem — xxvii
    The Book — xxix

Where Do You Begin? — 31

How Do You Get Materials for Your Classroom Library? — 39
    Building a Classroom Library with Homemade Books — 40
    Building a Classroom Library with Donated Books — 42
    Newspapers — 42
    Service Organizations — 42
    Nonprofits — 43
    Businesses — 43
    Garage Sales — 43
    Book Stores — 44
Post Office/AAA — 44
    Thrift Stores/Salvation Army/Goodwill — 44
    Friends of the Library — 45
    Junk Mail/College Info — 45

How Do You Create a Cozy, Inviting Library? — 49
    Focus on the Senses — 50
    Tastes — 51
    Smells — 51
    Sounds — 51
    Feel — 52
    Sights — 52

How Do You Make Reading Fun for Your Students? 61
Make a List of Strategies by Category 61
Environment 62
Talk 62
Content Knowledge and Class Systems 63
Writing 63
Games 64

What Do You Do Now? 73

How Do You Attract Volunteers? 77
Think Big 78
Use Your Students 79
Be Organized 79
Keep It Simple 79
Praise Publicly 80

Block 1: Talk 83

Block 2: Book Talk 87
A Typical Book Talk 90

Block 3: Picture Read 101

Block 4: Read Aloud 105
Read Aloud Guidelines 108
Preread 108
Rome Wasn't Built in a Day 108
Welcome Comments 108
Replay the Hits 109
Keep It Cozy 109
Have Fun! 109

Block 5: Partner Read — **113**

Block 6: Writing and Games — **123**

Time to Take Action — **129**

Appendix: Questions, Answers, and Checklists — **133**
   Block 1: Questions You Can Ask Students at Your
      First Meeting — 136
   Block 2: Book Talk — 137
   Block 3: Picture Read — 139
   Block 4: Read Aloud — 140
   Block 5: Partner Read — 143
   Block 6: Writing and Games — 145
   Six Blocks: Reading Session Organizational Structure — 147
   Six Blocks Blank Form — 148

References — **149**

FOREWORD

I was one of the first kids in my neighborhood to get engaged—I think I was around four or five. Even more amazing, I didn't even know I was engaged. I just thought I was looking at comic books. *Who knew?* We lived in an apartment house, no car until fifth grade, but a closet-full of comics and an encyclopedia in the living room with pictures of bombed-out buildings in Berlin and diagrams of people's intestines. Talk about engaging!

Which brings us to the freshest "buzz word" in reading circles: engagement. In 2000, an international study of a quarter million 15-year-olds from 32 countries showed those students who were the most "engaged" in reading had the highest literacy scores.* How does one measure engagement?

They were the students who read outside school most often, who read for pleasure as well as for school, who read the broadest cross-section of materials (magazines, newspapers, and fiction), and who came from the homes with the most print available and whose parents also were avid readers.

None of this should come as a surprise to anyone who knows the research and has been raising readers in a classroom or home. But it's a striking contrast with the mindset and mandated practices of the American classroom today. Anything smacking of pleasure or fun (like sustained silent reading) is demoted as nonessential. Anything above or below the class's reading level is either traumatizing or trivializing. If it can't be graded or won't be on the state test, forget it.

---

* Irwin Kirsch, John de Jong, Dominique LaFontaine, Joy McQueen, Juliette Mendelovits, and Christian Monseur, *Reading For Change: Performance And Engagement Across Countries, Results From Pisa 2000*, Organisation For Economic Co-Operation and Development (OECD), online at http://213.253.134.29/OECD/pdfs/browseit/9602071e.pdf.

We know that children who are the least engaged in school overwhelmingly come from homes where there are no reading role models and print is near to nonexistent. (There are a few exceptions to this norm and the author of this volume, Danny Brassell, is one of them, but he'll explain.) If the chances of the child catching the love of reading at home are slim to none, about the only place left is school, right? If we eliminate the chance in school, hope is doomed.

One of the most interesting things in the "engagement" study was that the lowest SES students who were the most engaged made the most improvement in scores and were the only ones to close the traditional achievement gap. With the mandated curriculum of "no child left untested," how can we turn reading into such a romantic experience that the child falls in love with it and gets "engaged"? Danny shows how to accomplish this.

None of this is theory to Danny Brassell. He's been there—disengaged as a kid and engaged as an adult. He's taught in some of the most deprived schools in America and he made them and his students richer by the day. He knows (and explains step-by-step here) how to meet the standards without turning your classroom into a boot camp. He's been a classroom teacher without even a dollar's budget, yet found ways to scavenge thousands of books—for free!

Danny also knows you can't catch a cold from someone who doesn't have one. And children cannot catch the love of reading from a teacher who doesn't have it either. If you're not an avid reader as an adult, how do you become one? Ask Danny Brassell.

What makes this book ironic is that when its author was a youngster, his family lived in a state that purged half of its libraries and staffs to save money, and thus his librarian-father lost his job. Today Danny Brassell's life is devoted to everything that state's purge tried to eliminate. You might say this book could be subtitled, "Revenge of the Librarian's Son." I'm certain you'll find it as engaging as I did.

—*Jim Trelease*
Springfield, MA
Author of *The Read-Aloud Handbook*

ACKNOWLEDGMENTS

I would like to thank Janice Gerson for all of her help in the preparation of this manuscript. She constantly inspires me with her generosity, marvelous ideas and timely feedback. Nestor Santtia, Sam Belmonte and the rest of the team for Go Habit Pro have made this a labor of love, and our work with international audiences ranks among the most rewarding of my life. My old colleague Cynthia McDermott provided numerous ideas and encouragement. Lois Bridges, Lynne Costa and the kind folks at Heinemann supported me before I ever gave a speech or wrote another book. I will always appreciate their support. I was lucky to get to work with a wonderful team at The Wonder of Reading which included Beth Michelson, Tarry Kang, Juliet Snowden, Phil Kligman and countless others who managed to get me in front of hundreds of audiences of adults and older siblings who wanted to help turn struggling and reluctant readers into more passionate readers. And to the legions of teachers, administrators, parents and reading volunteers who help me better understand what works and what doesn't with students, I want to express my profound gratitude. You've made me constantly curious and eager to find better ways to reach children. I still get excited when I see a disengaged student "light up" to learn something new.

PREFACE

So this book is really for two types of people. The first are the teachers in the trenches, dealing with students who come with diverse reading interests and abilities. This book will show you how to promote reading in ways that schools rarely do. And you'll learn how to economize your time by focusing on why students need to read rather than how to teach them to read. Don't get me wrong: teachers need to teach students how to read. But as I always ask audiences at my events: what good is it teaching kids how to read if they never want to read?

The other group of people are parents looking for ways to stoke a desire in their children to read. If you have a child who struggles with reading or shows little or no interest in reading, you will love this book. I show you all sorts of tricks that parents just like you have used to successfully engage their children to read more, read better and love reading. You will notice that the first five chapters lean heavily towards teachers. Who cares? Check them out, and see how you can adapt classroom strategies to fit your home. Oh, and please don't let the academic citations intimidate you. On the contrary, these are included to illuminate the extensive research that supports the ideas discussed in this book.

This should not be difficult. Simply grab what is meaningful to you, and run with it. If there is one thing I have learned in nearly 25 years as an educator, it is this: what is meaningful to one person may be meaningless to another. That's why we have to arm ourselves with plenty of weapons of mass instruction.

So, if you fall into either of those two categories, this book is for you. You are really going to enjoy the things that we cover in here. And you will be able to take all the value from it and use it to help your struggling student or reluctant reader become a more passionate and proficient reader.

Let's introduce our children to the joy of reading so that they make it a lifelong passion.

INTRODUCTION

*Reading is to the mind what
exercise is to the body.*

JOSEPH ADDISON

This is not your typical book on literacy. Unlike the dreaded textbook that provides the reader with stale statistics and antiquated strategies, this book inspires a permanent passion for reading. Reading should be fun, not work—devour this book with pleasure rather than use it as a sleeping aide by your bedside.

Reading is an essential component in maintaining a healthylifestyle. Too many people view opening a book like going to the gym: as a chore. Exercising your reading muscle is just as important as exercising the other muscles in your body. It rejuvenates you, makes you more attractive to others, and helps you live longer. Like eatinghealthy foods and going to the gym, if reading is practiced as a pleasurable activity, people will repeat the experience. By building on children's strengths and interests, you can motivate them to adapt reading workout habits. Each chapter of this book presents a component of a simple reading fitness program that encourages children to become readers for life.Let's introduce our children to the joy of reading so that they make it a lifelong passion. This book represents "the reading breakthrough" that helped shape www.ReadBETTERin67Steps.com, the world's leading reading engagement program that I developed.

THE AUTHOR

I developed this book based on my experiences working with students, teachers, parents, and administrators throughout the United States for the past 25 years. My passion for motivating people to read comes from my own embarrassing past—I was a reluctant reader growing up.

My father was a librarian, and I spent the majority of my adolescence doing whatever I could to stay away from books. Reading, to me, meant writing book reports based largely on *Cliffs Notes* and movie versions of literature. I had the occasional special teacher who motivated me to read this or that, but the majority of my reading was spent analyzing assigned topics that interested me about as much as catching a tropical disease. Assigned readings and book reports killed any potential interest I may have ever had in reading. Luckily, I did find my passion for reading, and it had to do with three experiences.

First, when I studied abroad in Spain as a college junior, I learned how difficult acquiring a second language can be. I had headaches from trying to think in Spanish all the time. I could choose two escapes: sniffing glue or reading books in English. I chose the latter— a girl loaned me her copy of John Grisham's *The Pelican Brief*, and I devoured it in one night. Then I breezed through *A Time to Kill*. I became so addicted to John Grisham while in Spain that I purchased a used English-language copy of *The Firm* for $27.

Later, when I graduated with my doctorate from the University of Southern California, I grinned from ear to ear. When my future wife asked me why I was so happy, my answer was simple. For the first time in my life, I realized that I would be choosing the books that I read. No more assigned readings!

Since graduate school, however, the dilapidated school systems where I have taught and supervised beginning teachers have done more to fuel my passion for reading than anything or anybody. I was fortunate enough when I was young to attend some great public schools with great public school teachers. They may have assigned dreadful reading assignments and required horrific book reports, but the public schools I attended provided plenty of resources. When I heard people gripe about the state of education in America, I could not understand their complaints. Therefore, when I began teaching in the inner city and witnessed firsthand how many students did not have adequate access to reading materials, I was infuriated. If we want students to become better readers, the least we can do is make sure they have plenty of reading materials available to them. I have dedicated myself to ensuring these forgotten students have fair access to the resources I enjoyed growing up. To that end, I now work with parents, teachers, and administrators on how to make reading a lifelong habit for students.

In organizing this book I wanted to create a simple metaphor for teachers – and when I say teachers, I mean all role models to children – to use when dealing with struggling and reluctant readers. In addition to a national reading crisis, the media has identified a crisis in physical fitness education. Hardly a day goes by without some report on young, obese couch potatoes addicted to cell phones, Big Macs, Ipads, Xboxes, and racy TV. If all of the media reports are right, the vast majority of youth in America are obese illiterates.

I believe both crises have been overexaggerated, but I also acknowledge that Americans have gotten lazy. Rather than point blame or discuss where society has failed, I wrote this book to identify solutions to get students to read for enjoyment. It is my hope that by making reading an enjoyable habit, students will be much more likely to read for pleasure outside of school on a more frequent basis.

THE PROBLEM

Why do kindergarteners anxiously go to bed with their backpacks the night before the first day of school, while so many sixth graders count the days until summer vacation? What makes a child turn from optimism and anticipation about learning to read to fear and dread? When does school turn from a game to a job in a child's mind? Is there a reason students who once applauded when their teachers announced it was time to read aloud a story now sit silently in fear of being asked to recite passages from their textbooks? I have taught students of all ages, shapes, cultures, and sizes and have been struck by students' regression and disillusionment as they progress from grade to grade.

And it's not just the students—enter any preschool or early elementary school classroom, and you will find a colorful atmosphere filled with music, laughter, finger paints, snacks, and naptime. As soon as sixth grade, if not earlier, classrooms become more orderly and neat, with rows and typed rules of procedure. Middle school teachers do not wear aprons with paint stains and snot marks. Show-and-tell is a distant memory. School has become all business. Smiley faces have been replaced with grade point averages.

Attending school for many students is like going to the gym for many adults: It is an obligation rather than a preference. What do we know about obligations? Most of us will delay them as long as possible or won't do them at all because we do not do things we hate. I wrote this book because I notice that by middle school many students hate reading, and we need to make reading fun for our students. Whether a teacher, parent, mentor, or coach, you can use the simple techniques in this book to make reading fun for them again. Reading should be like your favorite dessert: No matter how full you are, you can find room for it.

Why is reading so important? The research is clear: children who are not good readers have tougher lives. Over their lifetimes, they earn less money, are more apt to become depressed, and in general are not as healthy or fit as good readers. If children are to be fit readers, then, they need to have access to books that are fun, inspiring, and entertaining. Becoming a fit reader requires practice and access to the right kinds of materials. This book provides teachers and school leaders with clear, proven strategies to improve literacy curricula and implement a community volunteer program. Parents do not necessarily have to follow the system, but they will greatly benefit by implementing the ideas that I mention. I use a fitness program model that examines the materials needed to get started (research-based strategies on increasing book access and setting up a classroom library), a comprehensive reading program (a research-based tutoring program), and the resources and checklists to help you get your program started today. Are you ready? Set. Go!

THE BOOK

Providing access to reading materials and developing a dynamic library is integral to any classroom literacy program. Are you ready to begin a reading fitness program? In Chapters 1 through 5, I describe why children need books, and talk about teachers as reading fitness models. I hear many teachers say that they do not read because they don't have the time and don't really know where to start. Doesn't that sound like what you might say about an exercise program you wanted to start but didn't know how to begin? Think of reading for the teacher, the parent, the community, and the students as a lifelong activity that requires a little coaching, a little practice, and a few fits and starts in order to get those reading muscles lean and trim and ready for a long life. Your reading muscles are like any other muscles in your body: Inactivity prompts atrophy. Think of this book as your all-in-one gym that can create a lifelong passion in reading for you and your students.

In Chapter 6, I provide detailed, research-based strategies teachers can train volunteers to use with their students; I also tell you how to attract and train classroom volunteers. The Six Blocks program is a one-hour-a-week strategy that connects children with trained volunteers and engages them with books in the classroom. (I refer to it as a program simply to show that it is an easy-to-use process that can be adapted to a variety of settings.) I will even show you how to adapt the program to suit your particular program needs, as I have trained many ESL pull-out teachers how to fit the program into thirty minutes.

Chapters 7 through 12 introduce you to a fun, effective, and proven process—a reading fitness program—for getting your students involved with reading and for setting up your reading program correctly. Each chapter represents a ten-minute segment of the Six Blocks program. Chapter 13 provides final thoughts on why programs like Six Blocks are necessary, and why Six Blocks works.

If you are a parent, older sibling, concerned member of the community – whoever – don't be turned off that I talk about teachers and classrooms. No matter what you do, you are always a teacher and role model. Translation: adapt the ideas to meet your specific needs, and if you'd like an even clearer blueprint to help turn your struggling or reluctant reader into a more passionate and proficient reader, then you'll want to check-out www.ReadBETTERin67Steps.com, the world's leading reading engagement program. Many of the ideas for that program were formulated in my years developing the Six Blocks program for teachers and tutors.

Now you're ready to go! The appendix provides checklists and guides to keep you and your students on track to reaching your reading fitness goals. I have lots of experience supporting the success of the Six Blocks program, so the appendix also provides commonly asked, and my answers to, questions about the program.

So . . . lace up your jogging shoes and come along as I teach you how to transform your classroom into a reading fitness center!

CHAPTER

WHERE DO YOU BEGIN?

*If you think you are too small to make an impact,
try going to bed with a mosquito in the room.*

ANITA RODDICK

Why should you read? What should you read? Where do you find time? Who can help you? The basis for any good reading program rests with the teacher. Teachers need to model reading if they expect their students to read. If you are a teacher who would like to read but don't know how to get started, this chapter will coach you through strategies for becoming a practiced reader.

Sandy and Harry Chapin wrote a song a number of years ago called "Cat's in the Cradle." In the song a little boy grows up wanting to be just like his father. When he asks his father to play or teach him about life, however, his dad never seems to find the time for his son. Despite his father's neglect, the boy looks up to his father and tells himself that someday he wants to be just like his dad. As the son grows up into a young man, his father finally takes an interest in his son and wants to spend time with him. His son has become too involved in his own life, though, and cannot find the time to spend with his father. As the father reflects, he realizes that his son has grown up to be just like him: He has no time for him.

What kind of role model are you?

Are you a teacher who drills students with facts and ignores the interests of your students? Are you a coach who curses and cheats, or a mentor who downplays civic responsibility and advises children to look out for themselves? Are you a parent who returns home from a long, hard day at work and ignores your child in favor of the football game on television?

Take a moment and think about the best teachers you had throughout your lifetime. Now think about the worst teachers you had throughout your lifetime. My guess is that you did not fondly recollect teachers who boosted you up into the next quartile of standardized test scores. For most of us, the teachers who made a difference were the ones who took the time to pay attention to us and form relationships with us. Most of us do not remember what a teacher taught us or how they taught us. We remember how teachers made us feel.

I believe there are simple habits that we as adults can reinforce that will make a positive difference in the lives of children. Whether we like it or not, our actions have a significant impact on our children; we cannot take this responsibility lightly. We can make kids feel good about reading. While everyone understands the importance of reading, few acknowledge the everyday practices we model to our children. When a child sees role models who spend little time exercising, what is the likelihood that child will exercise? In the same respect, when students do not see teachers reading, they receive the message loud and clear: Reading must not be that important if the teacher never does it herself.

I believe in the power of little actions, as little things done by lots of people can make a big difference. Teachers and parents have an important responsibility that should never be taken for granted: We model the habits that our children will acquire for a lifetime. If we sit on the recliner, watch television, and devour fattening dinners every night, chances are that our children will grow up to do the same. Fortunately, if we eat healthy foods and perform daily exercise, our kids are more likely to acquire those habits.

I mentioned in the introduction that when I was a kid I despised reading. My parents jokingly trace the origins to when I was just over a year old and would sneak into my parents' bedroom. I'd take books off of their shelves and eat pages straight out of the books. My parents would slap me on the hands and say, "Stay away from the books, Danny. Bad boy!" Somehow, I like to joke, I believe these traumatic experiences prompted my negative attitude toward literature as a child.

On the other hand, my parents never really forced me to read. They'd occasionally buy me books that they thought I might be interested in, or they'd get me a magazine subscription to *Boys' Life* or *Sports Illustrated*. Beyond that, I rarely read aside from books that were assigned reading for school and menus at fast food restaurants. Still, I remember seeing my parents read tons of books, magazines, and newspapers every day. To this day, my mother reads aloud mail and newspaper articles that she finds interesting, even if they might not be that interesting to me.

Many people discourage kids from reading comic books or magazines or *Captain Underpants* because they do not feel the books are academic or serious. The fact is that the more reading of any kind that you do, the better you are going to get at it. A lot of folks don't believe walking is the most strenuous workout, but if you do enough walking you will significantly improve your stamina, burn calories, and reduce your risk for many diseases. You're more likely to take a jog if you have built up your walking. The same is true with reading. Before you give a kid a copy of James Joyce, why not hand him a copy of a *The Fantastic Four* comic book?

Later I'll talk about *why* you need books—now I'll talk about *who* needs to read. First off, teachers need to emphasize that reading starts in the home. For example, plenty of dads across the United States watch their favorite weekend sporting activities—they sit in front of the TV and shout with glee when their team scores and with disgust when they blow a play. Their total attention is on the game, and they devote an enormous amount of passion and energy into the exercise. Meanwhile, their child sits quietly ... and observes. How do you think this child is going to try to get his father's attention? As another stereotypical example, mom is in the kitchen cooking dinner and cleaning around the house. She is very involved in her activities. What are the children going to do to get their mother's attention? Now, consider mom and dad sitting down and reading books, newspapers, and magazines while listening to soft music. They read silently but occasionally tell one another about something interesting they just read. What kind of message is that sending to the child? Whoever the authority figures are in the home (I use *parents*, but that can mean foster parents, aunts and uncles, older siblings—any authority figures in the home), children observe their mentors.

Many people ask me where they should read with their students, and my answer is simple: *everywhere*. Parents listen to teachers, and teachers can point out some basic areas where parents can positively affect their children's reading habits. For example, Why not have a book basket on the breakfast table? Too many children are forced to read the backs of cereal boxes while they eat because there is nothing else available to read. And while many people will not admit it, the bathroom is a favorite reading space; why not install a little bookshelf with some interesting reading materials? What about beside the bed so they can read before they go to sleep? I confess that whenever I have trouble sleeping, I grab a handy education textbook or academic journal article to read. Those usually put me to sleep right away. On the other hand, I have stayed up half the night reading interesting novels because I couldn't sleep without knowing how the stories would end.

How about having things to read in the car? Advise parents to keep something handy in purses, briefcases, or backpacks so that whenever they are stuck in a line they have something to occupy their time rather than foster nasty thoughts about how much time they are wasting. Sounds like a pretty good idea for teachers, too— staff meetings always seem to go much more quickly when you bring a good book along. I perform some of my best reading at airports and on air- planes. I love airplanes because I can just sit and read a book. Of course, bring headphones so the person next to you does not feel compelled to tell you his or her life story from coast to coast while you try to read!

It is apparent that the best time to read is *all* the time. Soothing stories are a great way to calm children down at naptime. Exciting and inspirational stories are a great way to start the day. I read motivational books all the time because they make me feel good about myself and help me set goals. Maybe that's why the Bible is the best-selling book of all time—it makes people feel good and inspires them to do good things.

The most interesting question people ask me is what they should read, because typically people feel that as they get older they have to read more important literature. Baloney! I have said it before, and I'll say it again: Read whatever interests you. The more miserable stuff you read, the less you will enjoy it. The less you enjoy it, the less likely you are to do it for fun. Through research we know that people who read more, read better. So read a copy of *Cosmopolitan* magazine or a *Batman* comic. Settle down on the sofa and enjoy *Lady Chatterly's Lover* or your newspaper's sports page. Even President Gerald Ford said that when he was president he always read the sports page before the front page of the newspaper because the sports page celebrates man's accomplishments while the front page trumpets his defeats.

If you are teaching children how they should read, insist that they read in whatever manner makes them feel comfortable. Promote comfort by modeling what works for you and encouraging children to find the method that works best for them. Try sitting still without moving for ten minutes in an uncomfortable piece of furniture without talking to anybody. Sounds fun, right? Then why do so many teachers insist that students sit still during free reading time? Remember: Make reading a celebration. Turn on the tunes, and get the coffee brewing. Keep down the volume, but encourage movement. If a book is boring, put it down and pick up a new one. There are all sorts of great books out there, so don't waste your time reading lame books. Do you have a large book by your bedside that you started three years ago and still have not finished? I grant you permission to get rid of that book. Good readers discard books that don't interest them.

My biggest concern is that many teachers who are challenged to teach their students to read do not read for fun themselves. How is that going to work? If teachers do not have a passion for reading, they cannot ignite passion in their students. When I taught young students, I noticed that when I gave my students newspapers in class, the first section they would turn to was the weather map. It was not because that is the most interesting part of the newspaper; it was because I am interested in geography, and my students wanted to impress me with their geographical knowledge. Go around classrooms and find out what the teachers are interested in, and I bet there is always an abnormal proportion of students who are interested in that same activity. You have to model good reading habits by reading in front of your students. You need to read what you are interested in—even if it's considered "trash"—as that shows students that it's all right to read trash! (If you are reading this book you are obviously highly sophisticated and above reading such filth!)

Whenever I discover that teachers or parents or administrators are not reading anything for fun, I ask them why. They invariably offer the same pathetic excuse: "I don't have time to read anything." As a result of that discovery, I began to give audiences a few years ago recommendations of short literary works that anyone could read while waiting in a grocery line or sitting through a boring staff meeting. My goal: to stimulate people's interest in reading so that they make it a lifelong passion. What started as an email distribution list has evolved into a website, www.lazyreaders.com.

Each month I update the website with recommendations for quick, easy reads for personal pleasure. I try not to include any books over two hundred and fifty pages, and I always include books written for a variety of ages. See, adults should not be shy about reading children's books; they are some of my favorites because they generally have shorter chapters, bigger print, and colorful pictures. People who turn off the nightly news in favor of a good children's book probably live longer.

The website also includes an updated monthly list of my picks as well as archives of past selections by month, reading level, and page count. Also, books and other items purchased from amazon.com through links from the lazyreaders.com website directly benefit BookEnds (www.bookends.org), a nonprofit organization devoted to increasing children's access to books and community service awareness.

Essentially, there are many ways to get students interested in reading, but first you must show them that *you* enjoy reading. Take some time to find what you enjoy reading most. Chances are your students will pick up on that. When a book bores you, put that book down and find another. There are too many good books out there for you to waste your time on one that does not appeal to you. Finally, if you don't have time to read for fun, make a little time by carrying a short book with you to read while waiting in line.

Now you have a reason to become passionate about reading: The more you read, the more your students will read. Providing books is essential, so the next question is, "How do we get books for our classroom libraries?" Chapter 2 explores a variety of strategies that have worked for me.

MODELING IS IMPORTANT

Reading aloud to children is not the only important way of modeling reading behavior to children. Equally important is reading when students read (McCracken and McCracken 1978; Wheldall and Entwhisle 1988; Von Sprecken and Krashen 1998). When teachers read their own books of choice while providing students time to read their own books of choice, students see that reading is a pleasurable, lifelong activity. In effect, teachers need to model for students how reading is an enjoy- able routine (McCracken and McCracken 1978). Von Sprecken and Krashen (1998) found that whether the teacher reads while students read is an important factor in influencing whether students read during sustained silent reading (SSR). Finally, research by Wheldall and Entwhisle (1988) clearly shows that students read more when they see the teacher reading as opposed to cleaning up the classroom, grading papers, or eating lunch.

CHAPTER 2

HOW DO YOU GET MATERIALS FOR YOUR CLASSROOM LIBRARY?

*It is certainly true that you can lead a horse
to water but you cannot make him drink,
but we must make sure the water is there.*

STEPHEN KRASHEN

When I began teaching second grade in an underresourced school in 1994, my students had to learn without books. The school either had not been afforded sufficient funding for books or had not considered books an important part of their reading program. Whatever the reason, my class was given fewer than twenty textbooks for math, science, social studies, and music. Ironically, although the district expected me to boost my students' reading ability 1.6 years in eight months, I was handed three copies of the language arts textbook for my entire class of thirty-two students to share. I felt like I had been handed a couple of loaves of bread and some fish and expected to feed the masses.

Looking back, providing me with limited resources may have been the greatest favor my district ever did for my class: We had an opportunity either to make excuses or to solve problems, and we chose the latter.

BUILDING A CLASSROOM LIBRARY WITH HOMEMADE BOOKS

With endless learning objectives but limited resources, we made it our goal to create a classroom filled with books, magazines, newspapers, and whatever else we could get our hands on. Not only did I have to find reading materials—I had to find materials in Spanish and English. So I depended on my greatest resource—my students—and we began to make books ourselves.

The students and I made big books about our families, friends, and neighborhoods. We made little books to share with friends about pets, dinosaurs, and super heroes. We created classroom newspapers and bulletins about what we were doing in our classroom to share with the school and students' parents. *Somos autores* was our class motto: *We are authors.*

My students were good writers because they were becoming avid readers. Our classroom library became filled with magazines about the Los Angeles Lakers, storybooks about Ferdinand the bull, and newspapers with funny comic strips. Our library contained items in Spanish and English, with and without pictures. *Nuestra biblioteca* became the pride of our classroom, and my students anxiously showed off our library to the rest of the school.

Some of my colleagues could not believe what my class was doing. "You let kids sit together and fool around during reading time," one said. "You've got kids wandering around for ten minutes looking for a book to pick out." Another complained that my class was setting a bad example for other students. "Your kids read under the tables and on the floor, and some of them just read so they can play with stuffed animals."

My colleagues were absolutely right; my class was guilty of all of these accusations. My students had actually begun to *enjoy* reading. Many students asked to take a couple of books home each night.

Others stayed in the classroom during recess to read. While other classes completed worksheets on the letter *f*, my students created puppets of their favorite literary characters. If my students ever got bored with an activity, reading was always their favorite escape. "Your students read more than any other class on campus," my principal wrote on my evaluation, and, even though I am convinced he wrote that as a negative comment, I took it as a compliment.

The following year, I encouraged parents, relatives, and guardians to come to the classroom and read with students. I wanted to emphasize the importance of reading for students at home and at school, so I added a component to our student-made books: I asked parents to help students write stories in Spanish, their primary language. This idea came to me when, after receiving a large donation of books for our classroom library, I noticed a student looking bored with her copy of *Curious George*. I wondered why my students' interest in their new books had dwindled; I asked the little girl if she would read more books if they were in Spanish, and she and several of her classmates nodded vehemently.

When I asked parents at an after-school workshop in my classroom if they would be willing to help write and illustrate Spanish books with their children, they enthusiastically agreed. By allowing students to create books in Spanish with their parents, I believed that my students would be motivated to read more. Once our class started making books in Spanish, I observed that the donated English books in our library were more popular than ever, as many students liked to take the books home and create Spanish versions from them.

Students translated the Spanish books they created into English so that their classmates could practice at home and at school how to read both languages. Students who had not shown much interest in the classroom library before soon asked me to read books in Spanish and English from the classroom library so they could read the books at home. By the end of the year, our classroom was filled with students who chose to read for themselves and about themselves in order to better understand themselves.

BUILDING A CLASSROOM LIBRARY WITH DONATED BOOKS

There are a variety of ways to obtain free or substantially discounted reading materials for your classroom library. And don't let a lack of funding prevent you from upgrading your classroom library—following are just a few successful ideas I've used to obtain reading materials for my class and others' classrooms.

Newspapers

Most major newspapers have education representatives who can arrange for each of your students to receive free newspapers each week delivered to your school. In addition, newspaper education representatives usually provide packets of lesson planning ideas and ways for teachers to incorporate newspapers into their curricula. If you live in a large metropolitan area, you can obtain enough different newspapers so that each of your students receives one piece of free reading material each day! Newspapers are also excellent reading resources because they typically offer short articles on a variety of interests, and many offer children's sections and comics.

Service Organizations

Almost every community boasts a variety of service organizations, such as Rotary, Optimist clubs, and Lions clubs. Churches, temples, and veterans' organizations like the American Legion are also good places to ask for book donations. Some will provide checks for you to purchase books. It is worth every teacher's time to look into these organizations, because in addition to providing book resources, they are great places to enlist volunteers to read to your students.

Nonprofits

A variety of national nonprofit organizations specialize in providing books to teachers and students in need, including Reading Is Fundamental, First Book, and Rolling Readers. I have worked with a couple of wonderful literacy nonprofits in Los Angeles: BookEnds (www.bookends.org), which donates books directly to teachers, and the Wonder of Reading (www.wonderofreading.org), which creates school libraries and trains volunteers how to work on reading enjoyment with students. Every metropolitan area has a variety of literacy nonprofits that work with classroom teachers; rural areas also have a number of nonprofit foundations serving their interests and needs. Public libraries are often a good place to ask about the literacy non-profit organizations serving your particular community.

Businesses

By identifying yourself as a teacher, you almost always receive benefits. Many businesses will donate materials they do not need. For example, since my classroom did not have a rug for students to sit on while they read, I asked local carpet stores for any leftover carpets or carpet samples. Not only did I receive enough carpeting for my classroom, I received enough to carpet every classroom at my school and a couple others!

Garage Sales

When I first began teaching I spent just about every weekend at garage sales. They provide a perfect opportunity to see firsthand a community's goodwill. Whenever a person would point to a book and say it cost $5, I would perform my best Joe Friday imitation—I'd pull out my teacher identification card and say, "Well, I'm Danny Brassell, inner-city teacher. You know, my kids sure could use some books." Nine times out often, people would give me books for free; the other one time in ten people would give me a great deal. I'd always send a thank-you card with a photo of my class, and that worked better than a pyramid scheme. I would literally have those people and all of their friends calling me for years to pick up used books for my students.

Bookstores

Major bookstore chains offer up to 20 percent off on books for teachers, and many will donate damaged copies to teachers. Books without covers provide students with a perfect opportunity to show their comprehension of a story by designing their own book covers. Again, it is worth your time to build a relationship with your local bookstore, as many will provide students with bookmarks, old displays (one bookstore donated a life-size cardboard cutout of Harry Potter), and other promotional materials.

Post Office/AAA

Whenever a person moves and leaves no forwarding address, the post office holds that person's mail for a period of time. Ask your local post office if they will give you any unclaimed magazines; many will gladly comply. Additionally, many American Automobile Association (AAA) offices will donate used maps, pamphlets, and tour booklets to classroom teachers. Think of local agencies that are willing to give documents to your classroom. (One teacher asks her congresswoman to donate copies of bills and press releases to her classroom, and the congresswoman makes an annual appearance in the class to read to students.)

Thrift Stores/Salvation Army/Goodwill

These stores have supplied me with a ton of reading materials over the years for free or at greatly reduced prices when I described the lack of resources at my school. These establishments are also great at donating stuffed animals, cushions, and other items that can make your classroom library environment even more inviting. You'd be surprised how far a handwritten thank-you card from your students can go with cementing long-term friendships with businesses.

Friends of the Library

Almost every library has a Friends of the Library (FOL) chapter, and most FOLs hold annual book sales. Also, most FOLs receive hundreds of *National Geographic* donations and are glad to pass these along to teachers. FOLs love to give teachers materials for free or at greatly reduced prices, as many libraries have to dump books that go unused. The materials you get may be a little outdated, but it is always better to have something rather than nothing on your bookshelves.

Junk Mail/College Info

Another great way for teachers to help students flood their home environments with print is seeking out junk mail. I once worked with a third-grade teacher who complained that her students had nothing to read at home. So the two of us went to a few bookstores and public libraries and scanned travel and educational magazines for as many free information cards as we could find. The teacher then asked her third graders to fill out the postage-paid cards and send them in. Within a few weeks, her students received loads of mail on a daily basis. She also called several universities and received a ton of free materials for her third graders to read. While adults usually discard junk mail, imagine the look on a child's face when she receives several pieces of mail each day in her name.

One of the reasons I love working with teachers is because they are some of the most resourceful people I know. There is nothing that can stand in your way when you stand up for a worthy cause, and the literacy lives of your students depend on you. Get materials into your classroom for the sake of your students. As mentioned earlier, when seeking donations, remember two important things. First, *ask* for donations; second, write a class thank-you card for *all* donations. These two steps sound simple, but I am amazed by how often these two basic courtesies are ignored. These small gestures have garnered me tens of thousands of free reading materials for my classrooms and for others.

Now that you have ideas on how to get books and materials for your library, it is important to focus on ways to make your library a cozy, inviting place. Chapter 3 shows how you can make your classroom library the most awesome place in your classroom.

ACCESS TO BOOKS

In order to be able to read, students must have access to books. While often ignored as a matter of public policy or part of classroom curricula, it has been shown repeatedly (Brassell 1999; Dupuy and McQuillan 1997; Elley 1984; Elley 1992; Farris and Hancock 1991; Gaver 1963; Krashen 1998; Morrow and Weinstein 1986) that students who have greater access to books— and are permitted time to read these books—read more, and that increased reading leads to greater development of literacy skills such as comprehension, spelling, and vocabulary (Krashen 1988). Based on Krashen's reading hypothesis that "comprehensible input in the form of reading is the major source of literacy development" (1995, 187), it follows that the more exposure students have to books, the more reading they perform, which in turn leads to greater literacy development. Although access to books may not be a sufficient measure in increasing students' literacy abilities, it is certainly a necessary first step in improving one's ability to read, attitude toward literacy, and acquisition of language.

Early literacy experiences have been shown to vary greatly among different homes in different communities, however, especially in lower-income areas (Heath 1983; Snow, Burns, and Griffin 1998). Allington and Cunningham (1996) point out that several surveys of primary school teachers in the United States reveal that their greatest educational concern is the fact that many students, primarily those who are classified as being at-risk, are not yet "ready" when they enter school. Many students simply have much more limited experiences with books than others, causing them to have a disadvantage upon entering school. In essence, many students begin "the game" of school with points already on their scoreboard, while others try to play catch-up over the course of their schooling. The playing field is uneven from the opening gun.

Furthermore, many studies have shown how students from lower-income areas are negatively affected by limited literacy materials in their homes and daycare centers (Neuman 1999). A major discrepancy exists between "the haves and the have-nots" (Stanovich 1986). In several studies of students in developing countries (see Elley 1998; Greaney 1996), evidence clearly supports that increased access to books increases students' literacy capabilities. In the United States, the increased availability of books to students translates into better knowledge of vocabulary, comprehension, spelling, and general knowledge (Anderson, Wilson, and Fielding 1988; Stanovich and Cunningham 1992). "Book floods," programs that inundate educational facilities with increased book caches, have been shown to promote increased reading, which leads to greater improvements in literacy development (Elley 1992; Neuman 1999). This, in turn, leads to improved attitude toward reading and enhanced language acquisition.

CHAPTER

HOW DO YOU CREATE A COZY, INVITING LIBRARY?

*If you want to view paradise, simply look around
and view it. Anything you want to, do it.
Want to change the world? There's nothing to it.*

WILLY WONKA

Whenever I go into the gym, it seems that the staff have rearranged everything. Treadmills are pushed to the area formerly reserved for exercise bikes, elliptical machines occupy the old stretching mat area, and the free weights and machines have all been reorganized. The reason is twofold: Gym owners constantly want to make room for new equipment, and shuffling the exercise gear encourages patrons to visit different areas of the gym.

Organizing a classroom library needs to be just as strategic. Teachers need to constantly shift materials and draw student attention to different areas of their libraries in order to encourage full use. Where do you put materials? What is the optimal way to organize your classroom library? How do you create a cozy, inviting library?

When I was a boy, I hated libraries—after all, my father is a librarian, so I had to spend a lot of time in libraries growing up. I hated going to the library for a variety of reasons. For one, the libraries all smelled musky and stale. Librarians old enough to have known Christopher Columbus scolded me to be quiet. The furniture was uncomfortable. Also, all sorts of freaky people spent their time at the library—inevitably, anytime I walked into the library, a man thinking he was a vampire would haunt the aisles or some crazy lady would brush every book along her forehead. To me, as a child, libraries were eerie places.

Today, when I create classroom libraries, I model them on nice bookstores like Borders and Barnes and Noble. These places smell like coffee instead of vomit, they play soothing music rather than demonizing any form of speech, and they provide patrons with all sorts of cushy chairs and sofas to lounge on rather than hard, wooden stools. Bookstores like these have fared so well that many libraries have also grasped their ideas. You can find cafés, gift shops, and tons of computers in many libraries today, and often people visit libraries and bookstores to hear authors speak, enjoy concerts, or listen to poetry readings.

Nobody, outside of down-and-out prizefighters, will frequent gyms that are dingy, poorly lit, and filled with rotting equipment. The same is true for your classroom library. Don't expect a lot of kids to get enthusiastic about reading in a moldy corner with broken floor tiles, odors best not described, and books that seem to have survived the Civil War.

FOCUS ON THE SENSES

Because there are so many different media competing for children's attention today, we have to literally create classroom libraries that resemble interactive Disneylands. If we want to pull students' attention from their televisions and video games, we have to make classroom libraries that appeal to all of their senses.

Tastes

Why are we so afraid of children spilling? So many teachers and parents deny students the right to eat or drink around books because they are afraid the children will make a mess. It doesn't make sense! I have witnessed plenty of teachers allow students eating privileges in their classroom libraries. The key is to discuss with students the difference between a *right* and a *privilege,* and the clear expectation that while accidents happen, consistent spilling leads to no food or drink in the classroom library in the future. Students are very responsible when we give them responsibility; allowing a child the comfort of a snack and beverage is a great way of encouraging greater participation in your classroom library.

Smells

Mome teachers use scented candles and incense to mask the typically horrendous odors that make classroom libraries about as appealing as gas station restrooms. If you don't want to light any matches, air fresheners will also do the trick. I know a teacher who brews her coffee in her library corner. Another brings in pine needles and fresh flowers. People often say that smell is the sense that produces the most vivid memories, so why not invest in smells that make your classroom library appealing?

Sounds

If listening to Mozart can improve test scores, why not listen to music while reading? Music is such a powerful motivator for children, and I have watched teachers of all ages use music to attract students to their reading programs. By allowing students to select their own music while reading, we give them an added escape to use their imaginations. When I taught second graders, I was amazed how students who selected popular hip-hop songs at the beginning of the year turned to classical and jazz tunes by the end of the year. I asked students why they preferred musicians like Dizzy

Gillespie and Claude Debussy over Eminem and Snoop Dogg; they insisted that jazz and classical music helped them concentrate when they read. In fact, many students looked forward to reading time specifically because they knew they could listen to music. I have observed the same phenomena with students ranging from preschoolers to college undergraduates.

Feel

Hard floors and stiff chairs do not appeal to many people. If you want to get your students to hang out in your classroom library, you have got to provide cushions, carpet, stuffed animals, and any other items that are soft to touch. If so many of our struggling readers are kinesthetic learners, it only makes sense to provide them with comfortable items that they can touch. Providing pop-up and scratch-and-sniff books, along with books that come in different shapes, sizes, and styles, are ways to get students excited about the variety of reading materials available to them. They must first know that these different items exist, though. You can be the person that introduces variety to your students.

Sights

The look of your classroom library is the most important part of all. Most children look before they do anything, and a well-stocked and well-designed classroom library is sure to draw their attention. When I created school libraries for my own nonprofit project, I always based the library on a theme. At one elementary school, for example, I used Maurice Sendak's *Where the Wild Things Are* as our theme and turned the entire library into a jungle. I have seen teachers bring wading pools into their classroom libraries and allow students to fish for books with tiny plastic fishing poles. Another teacher brought a tent. Plenty of teachers bring sofas, cushions, stuffed animals, puppets, and props, such as hats, to make their classroom libraries popular hangouts for students. Put Christmas lights over your corner or hang student art projects overhead to make the library stand out. The point is, whatever you do, make the classroom library appear to be the coolest focal point of the classroom.

They say that it is better to give than to receive, and there is nothing more rewarding than creating a classroom library that your students love. Getting them interested in books is half the battle, and facilitating a wonderful environment will send the message to students that libraries are relaxing, comfortable, safe havens where they can escape their troubles in a world of books. Now that you have gotten students into your classroom library, though, it is time to make reading fun for them; Chapter 4 shows you how.

ACCESS TO BOOKS IMPROVES READING ABILITY

Those who have more books read more. Those who read more test better on measurements of comprehension, vocabulary, spelling, and questions of general knowledge. The earlier one is exposed to books, the greater the advantages. The research is clear.

Krashen (2004) quotes the adage that "it is certainly true that you can lead a horse to water but you cannot make him drink," but, he points out, that "we must make sure the water is there" (33). His review of studies concerning access to school libraries is straightforward and logical in its conclusion: The more books that are readily available to students, the more students read. In one of the first studies comparing the amount of reading materials present in school libraries with the literacy development of students, Gaver (1963) found that students who have access to a school library staffed with a librarian test better on vocabulary and reading skills measures than those who do not have access to a school library. In a study of school libraries throughout Quebec, Houle and Montmarquette (1984) showed that the actual number of books per student in school libraries is one of the most critical elements in determining student reading ability. Examining rural elementary schools throughout the United States, Farris and Hancock (1991) reported significantly higher reading scores in schools where the average number of books circulated per student exceeds thirty per year. Finally, a study of schools in Colorado (Lance, Welborn, and Hamilton-Pennell 1993) confirmed that the quality of a school library—defined by measures such as books, serials, videos per student, and total library staff hours per week—has a direct impact on student reading achievement scores, specifically on the Iowa Test of Basic Skills.

The school library is not the only source for books in a school; several studies have shown the effects of increased book stocks in classroom libraries. Comparing elementary students' various uses of classroom libraries, Powell (1966) determined that students with greater access to books in classroom libraries read more frequently than those with less access, which in turn leads to better student performance on tests of reading ability. So-called book flood approaches, programs designed to significantly increase the number of books in a classroom, have also shown the positive effects on reading ability resulting from a rise in reading materials (see Elley 1998). Through his involvement in book flood programs in developing Third World countries, Elley (1998), perhaps more than any other researcher, has proven repeatedly the value of increased book access on reading ability in the classrooms of students throughout the world in places like Sri Lanka, South Africa, and Fiji. In every international classroom he has flooded with books, Elley has concluded that increased access to books positively affects students' reading ability.

Because measures of word recognition, vocabulary knowledge, and reading comprehension are among the most insightful indicators of students' reading ability, it is important to understand that increased reading, as a result of increased access, leads to better student performance on all of these skills areas (Nagy, Herman, and Anderson 1985). The more students read books, the better they perform on measures of reading comprehension, vocabulary, and reading speed (Anderson, Wilson, and Fielding 1988). Also, if increased access to reading materials leads to increased reading, it has been found that one's verbal fluency, spelling, and knowledge of general information will all be enhanced (Cunningham and Stanovich 1998). Finally, Cunningham and Stanovich (1998) argue that students who are exposed to reading at a younger age are more likely to make reading a lifetime habit, inevitably improving their reading abilities.

Children's reading abilities improve when they are exposed to books at an early age. It is never too early for caregivers to start promoting literacy habits with children (Barclay, Benelli, and Curtis 1995). When students are provided with a greater availability of books in their classrooms, it is argued, they are able to better develop their emergent literacy skills (Taylor, Blum, and Logsdon 1986). In a longitudinal study of preschool students, Tobin and Pikulski (1988) determined that early exposure to literacy activities such as books leads to future literacy benefits. Kindergartners who are provided with greater access to books score higher on tests of comprehension and original story creation (Morrow and Weinstein 1982), and first graders exposed to more books have been observed performing better on tests of reading ability as well (Gambrell 1996). In effect, students who are exposed to more books at an earlier age show greater reading ability than those with limited exposure, and this increased exposure to interesting reading materials enhances students' desire to read.

ACCESS TO BOOKS IMPROVES READING ATTITUDE

Provided students have access to books that they are interested in (for example, those with exciting subject matter, visual appeal, and those written in their primary language) and are allowed to choose and discuss books on their own, the increased access improves reading attitude. However, access is not enough in improving reading attitude. It is vital that students be encouraged to access books, and that students who do not yet read conventionally, such as emergent readers, be read to by their teachers and other adults.

Because children live in households where the amount of reading materials and literacy experiences (reading a storybook with a parent, looking at labels on cans) may vary greatly, teachers need to make sure to provide as many literacy experiences as possible. Exposure to books is a critical first step in motivating students to read, and empowering students to read voluntarily seems to teach children to connect reading with pleasure. Morrow points out that "if youngsters enjoy looking at books, then eventually reading them, they will tend to read more, which in turn can lead to improved reading ability" (1991, 681). And Cunningham and Stanovich (1998) claim they cannot overstate the importance of providing young students with books, pointing out that creating interest in reading at an early age can lead to a lifetime of reading experiences.

Two motivations seem to be most important in explaining how increased access to books can improve one's reading attitude: reading for knowledge and reading for pleasure (McEvoy and Vincent 1980). Books that cover topics of interest for students are needed if students are to read for either knowledge or pleasure. The greatest indicator of how increased exposure to books improves one's reading attitude can be found in studies of students' reading frequency. A plethora of research (Brassell 1998, 1999; Constantino 1995; Krashen 2004) indicates that when students are allowed access to more books and permitted time to read them, they read more. When given the chance to read more books on their own, children have been found to read more—further emphasizing the importance of early exposure on reading attitude (Neuman 1999).

For the child who may not have access to books at home, schools are crucial in providing reading materials that can attract these children to what has been called one of the world's most exclusive and beneficial clubs, "the literacy club" (Smith 1988).

ACCESS TO BOOKS IMPROVES LANGUAGE ACQUISITION

Many researchers are adamant in their belief that access to books is crucial to language development, as books provide substantially greater proportions of vocabulary than children ever encounter through natural speech (Hayes and Ahrens 1988; Nagy, Herman, and Anderson 1985; Stanovich 1986). Compared to written language, oral language is a desert in terms of exposure to new words, or words that have not yet been encountered. Cunningham and Stanovich point out that "the relative rarity of the words in children's books is, in fact, greater than that in all of the adult conversation, except for courtroom testimony" (1998, 426). Selected statistics for major sources of spoken and written language (Hayes and Ahrens 1988) reveal that children's books contain more than 50 percent more rare words than standard television programming. Hayes and Ahrens (1988) found that almost 95 percent of words used on television and in conversation are from the five thousand most frequently used; it is clear that a person's vocabulary extends beyond the most frequent usages as a result of the significant influence of reading books.

The availability of books is a crucial element in a child's language development. Of particular importance to a child's first language development is the availability of books in his or her primary language, especially when considering the needs of students who come from low-income homes in the United States, many of whom are nonnative English speakers who hail from different countries. Cummins (1991) advocates for primary language materials to enhance primary language skills—he shows that the development of primary language benefits academic achievement. One of the best ways, then, that our schools can assist second language learners in acquiring English is by first exposing them to a variety of materials in their primary language. As Cummins argues, a program that promotes literacy activities in children's primary language enables children to enhance their first and second language proficiency. In fact, denying children access to reading materials in their primary language could prove to have detrimental effects on their literacy in their first and second language (Snow 1990).

Greater access to books benefits students who are trying to acquire a language other than English, as well. Elley's research (1998) on international students' increased exposure to printed materials in English showed that it benefits all aspects of children's language growth. Krashen (2004) argues that books provide second language learners with crucial comprehensible input that enables them to easily acquire a second language. For younger children who may not yet be able to read conventionally, increased access to books—such as read alouds with a teacher—is an essential aspect in developing their ability to communicate.

Although research demonstrates how students first need access to books in order to improve their reading ability, reading attitude, and language acquisition (among other things like general knowledge and behavior), it is important to note that access to books is not the sole component of a successful reading intervention for children at any age.

CHAPTER 4

HOW DO YOU MAKE READING FUN FOR YOUR STUDENTS?

There is more treasure in books than in all the pirate's loot on Treasure Island.

WALT DISNEY

MAKE A LIST OF STRATEGIES BY CATEGORY

Teachers always ask me how they can make their libraries the central focus of literacy in their classrooms. One afternoon I developed a list of 132 strategies for teaching reading, and I am sure I could think of another 132 if I needed to. The point is that all of these strategies are designed to instill a passion for reading in each student. (See pages 66–71 for the complete list of numbered strategies.)

This list is by no means a finalized list, as people constantly provide me with new strategies to add to the list. At first glance, the list can seem a bit overwhelming, so I categorized strategies so that teachers, parents, and volunteers could better grasp ways to get students interested in reading. I list the number of each strategy in parentheses after I mention it below.

Environment

Chapter 3 provided a detailed overview of ways to create a cozy, inviting library (2, 3, 34, 46, 129). Beyond that, students enjoy supplying a lot of environmental print (49) for their classrooms in the form of cereal box covers, signs, wrappers, and so on. In fact, the more students create the print in the classroom, the more likely they are to look at that print (40, 102). The classroom library should host a variety of different materials (4, 16, 18, 41, 57, 65, 66, 79, 83, 101, 114), and you should allow students to choose what they'd like to read and give them time to read (1, 5). You should read while the students read (35), and place baskets of books (48) on students' tables so they can easily exchange books without bothering you or anyone else. Make reading fun by reading ghost stories with flashlights (19) and providing students with puppets and stuffed animals to read with (20, 96). Listening centers (77) and computers (45) are always popular, and highlighting students' dioramas (100) and words that they contribute to the word wall (90) also help promote print in the classroom.

Talk

Teachers can make a significant difference in their students' reading interests by reading aloud great stories (6, 7, 21, 22) and leading inter esting book talks (9, 10) where students can discuss stories (32, 39, 111), analyze story features (76, 80, 85, 122, 126), and make predictions (23, 30). The morning meeting (97) is another great opportunity for teachers and students to talk about books. Making time for students to tell jokes and riddles (81), interview one another (121), and share personal items during show-and-tell (116) are also strong motivators. I used to ask students to record themselves reading aloud books (119), and my other students could listen to the tapes or they would give the tapes to classes with younger readers. I also led a daily People's Court ritual (128) where students would role-play as if they were in a courtroom and discuss any disagreements or problems they may have had with one another throughout the day.

Content Knowledge and Class Systems

Teachers can turn students on to reading by integrating reading throughout their daily routines and showing students ways reading can enhance student knowledge in different content areas. By reading to and with students and showing students they can improve comprehension by looking at pictures in stories and rereading stories (11–14, 31, 69, 70, 72), teachers can facilitate less stressful reading environments. An easy way to get students interested in stories is to find stories with characters that have the same names as your students (15). Encourage students to keep reading materials handy so they are never bored (132) and monitor their progress by keeping track of all the words they read each day, week, month, and year (131). You can encourage the importance of reading by taking students to the public library to get their library cards (36) and encouraging volunteers to come read to your class or with specific students (44, 78). Teachers can teach students tricks to enhance their comprehension, vocabulary, and fluency (17, 54–56, 62, 64, 75, 82, 84, 123, 125) and reward students with reading time (33). By integrating reading into all classroom activities, teachers demonstrate to students the importance and usefulness of reading.

Writing

If students want to become good writers, they have to become readers. There are a variety of ways of using writing to make reluctant students read more willingly. Whenever students create the materials in a classroom, they are more likely to use those materials (28, 29,

88, 89, 91, 94, 103–105). I have observed many teachers engage students in writing sequels to stories they enjoyed (24), dictating stories (26), and creating song lyrics (42). There are a number of fun, silly writing activities that promote student reading, such as writing silly questions for the teacher (47) and creating their own words, known as Sniglets (50), or writing analogies, idioms, recipes, poetry, or Mad Libs (51–53, 58, 74). Students often benefit from keeping track of their daily experiences in journals, planners, and diaries (86, 106, 117) and by corresponding with one another or people far away (87, 98). Again, students are more likely to read their own writing, so allowing students to rewrite stories in their own words (130), maintain their own portfolios (118), and create résumés (121) are excellent ways to boost students' reading opportunities.

Games

Finally, there is no better way to get kids to do anything than to make it into a game. Many students love to perform, so create a number of arenas for them to get up and act like characters from books they have read or written (25, 67, 68, 99, 115, 120). Students love anything that involves clues, so scavenger hunts (38), coded messages (63), and treasure maps (107) are a great way to get students reading. Board games (8) are always popular, as are word games like crosswords (27), concentration (59), hangperson (60), word jumbles (71), and word finds (110). Songs and chants (73) get students up out of their seats, as do total physical response activities (109). Just remember that as long as you can turn a task into a game, students will be interested in it.

Reading should always be a fun activity, otherwise there is no way students are going to be drawn to it repeatedly. I observe teachers every day who have a variety of wonderful ideas they use to promote reading with their students. The more strategies you have up your sleeve, the higher the probability that you will get through to each and every student. Keep in mind that schools were built for students, not teachers, and we have to make accommodations that benefit students. In Chapter 5, I will show you what to do now that you have your materials and strategies at hand.

132 STRATEGIES FOR TEACHING READING

1. Make time to read.
2. Find a cool place to read.
3. Get cool things to read.
4. Get different types of items to read (books, magazines, menus, cereal boxes, and so on).
5. Encourage freedom of choice (allow kids to select what they want to read).
6. Read aloud.
7. Be read aloud to.
8. Play board games.
9. Give teacher book talks (the salesperson technique).
10. Discuss readings with friends (literature circles).
11. Read in stereo (partner read).
12. Do a popcorn read, without the stress.
13. Enjoy a picture read.
14. Repeat readings.
15. Find stories with characters that have names of your students.
16. Read easy books.
17. Facilitate crosscurricular themes.
18. Read tough books.
19. Read ghost stories with a flashlight.
20. Read to a stuffed animal.
21. Read with funny voices.
22. Make sounds for different characters when a story is read aloud.
23. Ask students to guess the ending.
24. Ask students to write the sequel.

25. Allow students to perform as different characters.
26. Dictate stories.
27. Tackle crosswords.
28. Ask students to write their own books.
29. Create classroom Big Books.
30. Ask students to guess what the story is about based on title and cover.
31. Use Big Books and follow text with finger.
32. Ask lots of questions, no book reports or tests.
33. Reward students with reading time.
34. Create an awesome classroom library.
35. Read while students read.
36. Take students to the public library and make sure they all get library cards.
37. Ask parents to turn on closed captioning on their televisions.
38. Conduct scavenger hunts!
39. Ask students to brainstorm as many things they can think of that require reading. Whoever can think of the most gets a free book.
40. Prepare class labels.
41. Call your local newspaper and ask for classroom editions so all students have newspapers to take home.
42. Sing song lyrics.
43. Take advantage of rain gutter bookshelves.
44. Research celebrity readers.
45. Take advantage of your classroom computers.
46. Get students on junk mail lists.
47. Ask students to write silly questions that they can put into a hat. As an end-of-day incentive, the teacher or a student draws a question and answers it as wisely as possible.
48. Have book baskets readily available at students' desks so they can read when they finish activities early.

49. Encourage environmental print in the classroom.
50. Allow students to create their own Sniglets.
51. Create analogies.
52. Create idioms.
53. Follow instructions/recipes.
54. Teach clues (e.g., initial or final sound, rhymes with, look at picture).
55. Teach context cues.
56. Teach K-W-L Plus.
57. Keep plenty of dictionaries on hand.
58. Use commercial Mad Libs or create your own.
59. Play the game of Concentration.
60. Play Hangperson.
61. Play Scrabblegrams.
62. Create cliff drawings (sequence of events).
63. Create coded messages.
64. Encourage speed reading for informational texts (headings, subheadings, highlighted words, chapter summaries).
65. Read nursery rhymes and fairy tales.
66. Find stories about your students' culture, and environment.
67. Write Author invitations (Hot Seat).
68. Designate a favorite book character dress-up day.
69. Encourage readers' theatre.
70. Use guided reading.
71. Play word jumbles.
72. Work on shared reading/choral reading.
73. Read, write, and perform songs and chants.
74. Read lots of different types of poems.
75. Revisit, reflect, retell stories.
76. Role play.
77. Create books on tape/listening centers.

78. Establish book buddies and reading volunteers.
79. Play Leap Frog.
80. Engage in reciprocal teaching (summarize, question, clarify, predict).
81. Tell jokes and riddles.
82. Use Venn diagrams.
83. Read comic books.
84. Use semantic webs and maps.
85. Compare and contrast characters, stories, and so on.
86. Keep a journal or a learning log about what you're reading.
87. Share letters, messages, and notes.
88. Create book covers and bookmarks to promote books.
89. Make word cards.
90. Make word walls.
91. Create words with affixes and roots (morphemic analysis).
92. Create a class checkout system with student librarians.
93. Play bingo with words, characters, stories, and so on.
94. Create a sentence construction zone using pocket charts.
95. Engage kinesthetic learners with magnetic letters, Silly Putty, and so on.
96. Use puppets and stuffed animals.
97. Make use of morning meeting and announcement time.
98. Find a pen pal.
99. Play charades.
100. Create dioramas.
101. Read pattern books.
102. Create alphabet cards with pictures and realia.
103. Create classroom newsletters, cards, and invitations.
104. Create math word problems.
105. Engage in classroom responsibilities, such as monitoring attendance.
106. Create grocery lists and day planners.

107. Create directions (e.g., treasure maps).
108. Find words that (start with *j*, have two syllables, rhyme with can, and so on).
109. Use total physical response (clap the number of syllables in pumpkin, and so on).
110. Create word finds.
111. Generate a class list of why students like to read.
112. Play Slug Bug and other car games.
113. Use word wheels (e.g., letters of alphabet + word endings like -an).
114. Read chapter books.
115. Create plays (ghost stories, folktales, legends, and so on).
116. Play show-and-tell.
117. Keep personal teacher–student diaries for all students.
118. Keep student-maintained portfolios.
119. Allow students to record themselves reading stories.
120. Using light from an overhead projector, "shine the spotlight" on students willing to announce their favorite parts of a story.
121. Create résumés, job applications, and mock interviews.
122. Ask students to discuss how different characters might react to hypothetical situations (e.g., What if the Little Red Hen had help?).
123. Use the 3-2-1 strategy (3 things you learned, 2 interesting things, and 1 question you still have).
124. Discuss concepts about print.
125. Create jigsaw puzzles.
126. Modify the text (e.g., retell the story and put into your own words).
127. Create a classroom mailbox.
128. Role-play the People's Court (discuss problems in a mock-courtroom setting).
129. Fish for information using a wading pool and toy fishing poles.

130. Rewrite stories into the current environment (e.g., Little Red Riding Hood in Los Angeles).
131. Keep track of the amount of text the class reads—up to a million words.
132. Engage in line reading.

CHAPTER

WHAT DO YOU DO NOW?

A journey of a thousand miles begins with a single step.

CONFUCIUS

Congratulations! You have created a wonderful classroom library filled with high-interest reading materials, comfortable seating, and an inviting atmosphere. Access is not enough, though. Just because you purchase a gym membership doesn't mean you will go to the gym. Have you ever noticed how packed most gyms are in January and how many fewer people can be spotted working out in April? Every year people make a list of New Year's resolutions that they enthusiastically pursue in January and lose interest in within a couple of months. The secret to sustainability is creating a program that provides access, motivation, and accountability. How can you ensure that students not only use the classroom library but also benefit from the library?

I have found that there is no greater epidemic than apathy. Apathy kills. It kills dreams, effort, and follow-through. Apathy signifies lack of interest, and I learned long ago that there is a great way to defeat apathy: Support.

Have you ever run a marathon? I have run in four and finished three. True, I did not set any world records, but I must point out that 26.2 miles is no walk in the park (rather, it is more like thirty walks in the park performed back-to-back on the same day). It is a significant test of physical fitness. What I learned from running marathons, though, is that the toughest threshold to cross is not the finish line but the mental wall. By the twelfth mile of the race in my first marathon, I began questioning my sanity for entering such a death march. By mile sixteen I had effectively convinced myself that I could not finish, and I dropped out of the race. The sting of that failure bothered me for several months, and I decided to enter the same marathon the following year.

The next time I ran in the marathon, however, I asked some friends to join me. I trained with my friends for a couple of months and drove along the route of the marathon to mentally prepare for the race before we ran it. When we ran the marathon together, I hit the mental wall again. This time I did not hit the wall until mile sixteen, but with support and encouragement from my friends, I focused on finishing the race. All three of us finished together, and I went on to race in two more marathons.

The point of the story is not to prove my physical endurance, although many have claimed I stand as a striking specimen. What I learned is that anything worth doing is made a lot easier with the support and encouragement of others around you. If we are going to create lifelong readers, we have got to read ourselves. We need to support our children's efforts in reading the way parents attend children's sporting events.

What are some strategies?

In order to support children's reading efforts, we need to create support teams. Parents, siblings, and other influences in the home are essential in this process. Unfortunately, for a variety of reasons, the home cannot always be depended on to adequately support students' literacy, so outside influences also need to be considered. Teachers play an integral role in each child's literacy, but with so many students in the classroom, a lot of teachers cannot provide enough one-on-one attention. Therefore, another source needs to be considered: Volunteers.

Over the past dozen years I have traveled the world and spoken to over 2,500 audiences ranging from teachers and parents to government and business leaders. My mission is to share a joy of reading that infects others. I have been humbled to have met so many wonderful leaders who have helped me understand the importance of reading in every person's development.

One of the greatest experiences of my life was training thousands of parents, teachers, community volunteers and older siblings work one-on-one with struggling and reluctant readers. Working with these marvelous heroes I tried to make it as clear as possible that making a difference in the lives of our students requires the support of everyone in our communities.

What most people do not understand though, is that it takes only a brief amount of time over a sustained period of time to make a substantial difference. An hour a week of one-on-one time with a student over a six-month period works in much the same way as stopping by the gym a couple of times a week: In six months, you are going to look at yourself in the mirror and be a lot happier by what you see. And, in my experience, the wonder of volunteering is that volunteers benefit as much as the students with whom they work.

To be successful in any program—whether preparing for a marathon or learning to read—we need support. We know that we are more likely to go to the gym if we are going to meet a trainer or friend there. The same is true with reading volunteers: Accountability matters. Chapter 6 describes how teachers can recruit volunteers of all ages and from an array of sectors to help students develop their reading interests. Teachers cannot do it alone—you need to enlist the support of your community, and then you will see what an impact you truly can have on your students.

CHAPTER

HOW DO YOU ATTRACT VOLUNTEERS?

*Ask not what your country can do for you,
ask what you can do for your country.*

PRESIDENT JOHN F. KENNEDY

There are so many worthy causes in society, from working with the homeless to promoting environmental conservation. One of the great aspects of childhood literacy is that no matter what political views you have, pretty much everyone can agree that assisting students in reading is important. While different methods of promoting literacy may be controversial, the goal of literacy is not. As a result, recruiting literacy volunteers is easier than recruiting volunteers to pass out campaign flyers or to preach the teachings of their religion. That said, attracting volunteers for your reading fitness program is by no means an easy task.

Of course, parents and relatives are the first people we strive to attract to our classrooms. Unfortunately, many parents work long hours and/or multiple jobs, and they cannot participate in classroom programs as much as they'd like. The next best option is to recruit volunteers, or peer tutors, from a higher grade level. For example, I have paired many fifth graders with second graders. Peer tutoring is a strong strategy because, among other things, it aids the second grader in developing his reading skills while reinforcing reading concepts in the fifth grader.

Beyond families and schools, the community offers a variety of volunteer options. Many businesses allow their employees to take an hour or two a week to participate in community service programs. I have had success at recruiting workers from car dealerships, telephone companies, restaurants, and hair salons, among others. Many public agencies are also very involved in their communities. Police officers, firefighters, librarians, and politicians make great reading partners. Also, if you have a university or other college in your community, enlist college students to work with your kids; many colleges will provide academic units for such service-based learning. The Americorps program even pays volunteers a stipend.

The key to attracting volunteers is persistence. While anyone can place a photocopied flyer on a bulletin board or a short announcement in a newspaper, the response rates on these methods are negligible. If you really want to recruit volunteers, you have to do a little work; it will pay big dividends for you and your students in the long run. I have some ideas that I hope you find to be helpful.

Think Big

One of my favorite quotes to tell students is "little things done by lots of people make a big difference." The same philosophy applies to volunteer recruitment. Call this the Sally Struthers approach—actress Sally Struthers used to make pleas on television for people to donate the equivalent of what it would cost for a cup of coffee a day to help provide food for impoverished children around the world. The same approach can work for your reading fitness program. When people stretch for five to ten minutes a day or take short walks, they feel better. Volunteering an hour a week with a child—the equivalent of twelve minutes a day during a work week (or the time it takes most people to have a morning coffee break)—can lead to igniting a child's passion for reading that could last a lifetime.

Use Your Students

Children are the most powerful salespeople in the world. If you feel uncomfortable recruiting volunteers, enlist your students' help. Adults are much less likely to hang up or slam the door on a child. Time and again I have seen students enroll the help of volunteers through heartfelt pleas. I know a teacher who brings a student with her every year to speak to the local Rotary Club and chamber of commerce, and she always has so many people call her to volunteer that she passes along volunteers to her fellow first-grade teachers.

Be Organized

Anyone can ask for help. Too often, unfortunately, I have seen teachers successfully recruit volunteers and then unsuccessfully use them. Make sure you have a program in place that you, your principal, and your students all understand. There is nothing worse than getting a person to volunteer his or her time to help and then not knowing where, when, or how they can read with a student. The better organized you are, the easier it will be to get people on board to assist you.

Keep It Simple

Teaching reading is not easy. Teaching a love for reading is. Volunteers do not require certification, because they function as inspirational mentors to students. If you want to help your volunteers make reading comfortable for their students, you need to promote a program that is easy for volunteers to understand. My typical volunteer training occurs once for approximately two-and-a-half hours, and my volunteers leave feeling invigorated and empowered. I make sure to emphasize that volunteers are not expected to teach students reading strategies or decoding skills—that's the teacher's responsibility. Instead, I make it clear that volunteers only need to make reading a very fun and positive experience for their students.

I always point out that volunteering is sort of like being an aunt or an uncle: You get to have all the fun and then stick the parents (or, in this case, the teacher) with all the nitty-gritty work.

Praise Publicly

Even though volunteers donate their time to work with students so that they can help children improve their literacy skills, you have a better shot at retaining and expanding your volunteer base by acknowledging your volunteers' efforts. Write a personalized thank-you letter to every volunteer and insist that students write thank-you letters, too. It doesn't cost a lot of time or money to invite all volunteers at the end of a semester to a potluck celebration. Ask students to make presentations, allow administrators to address the volunteers, and provide each volunteer with a certificate and small gift. One teacher I have worked with always gives each volunteer a laminated studentmade bookmark, a certificate of appreciation, and a framed photo of each volunteer working with a student. Thanks to donations and discount stores, she can make goodie bags for all of her volunteers that cost less than five dollars per volunteer. She has never lost a volunteer in her three years running her reading buddies program, and she has successfully shown colleagues at her school and in her district how to recruit and retain their own volunteers.

The benefits of getting volunteers to come to your classroom go way beyond your reading program. Students need to see how important their achievement is to the community, and a steady stream of classroom volunteers promotes student interest in all academics and encourages students to provide their best effort. When communities envelop students with care and concern, students rise to expectations. Like personal trainers or workout partners at the gym, reading volunteers provide students with accountability.

A simple volunteer reading program can do wonders for students' reading attitudes and aptitudes. In Chapters 7 through 12, I break down six specific strategies that volunteers can use with their students. Each chapter focuses on a ten-minute period, or block, and specifically acknowledges the research that supports each strategy. I call this the Six Blocks program, in which volunteers work with struggling readers for an hour a week over a six month-period. Blocks include speaking with students, conducting book talks, venturing on picture reads, reading aloud, partner reading, and writing with students, all in ten-minute blocks, a format proven to be highly effective, engaging, and successful.

Teachers can use the Six Blocks program with their students, but the point of Six Blocks is to recruit volunteers to work one-on-one with students. Therefore, keep in mind that all tips offered are meant to be used with students on an individual basis, not in groups. The strength of the program rests with the consistent individual attention each student receives in realizing the magic of books.

CHAPTER

BLOCK 1: TALK

I love talking about nothing.
It's the only thing I know anything about.

OSCAR WILDE

The simplest activities are generally the most important activities. I believe that every hour that you work one-on-one with your student you should set aside some time to talk with him or her. Consider the first block in the Six Blocks program the "stretching" portion of your reading fitness program.

When building a fitness regimen, many people work with a trainer. Although it's true that trainers offer a wealth of expertise in proper exercise and dietary habits, one of the trainer's most important functions is to provide motivation and accountability. Pupils are more likely to stick with a program when they know that somebody else depends on them to show up.

Speaking and listening are highly underrated skills, especially since many students come from predominantly oral backgrounds—those who read and write the least are often the most proficient speakers and listeners. Spending time each session getting to know your student and letting her get to know you can prove invaluable when determining the interests and needs of your student. Informal dialogues often establish an easygoing rapport with children that shows them you care.

The first time you talk with your student, you are on a mission to find out as much as you can about him or her. Try to find out what turns this kid on. The more you know about your student, the better chance you have of providing a high-quality experience that will secure his or her inclusion into what educator Frank Smith calls the literacy club. Passionate readers read for life, and I want you to enable students to become passionate readers.

Also, remember that children are just as interested in you as you are in them. In fact, the more you open up to your students, the more they will open up to you. Around the third time I meet with students is when I get out my old naked *baby* photos. (Remember, baby photos. If you show naked photos of yourself as an adult, you will probably— and hopefully—be prosecuted.) In all seriousness, it is important for you to talk about your own trials and tribulations growing up so that kids understand that everyone experiences difficult phases and dilemmas. I tell the students I work with how I hated reading growing up; I try to determine what types of materials students prefer, be it books or magazines, comics or newspapers. Keep in mind that gyms have exercise bikes and treadmills and stair climbers and rowing machines because different equipment attracts different patrons. You want to ask a lot of questions to determine what reading equipment best suits your student so that he or she will stick with your program.

So what questions do you ask? Good journalists know that the questions you ask start with are *who, what, when, where, why,* and *how*. Ask a "yes" or "no" question and you should expect to receive "yes" or "no" answers. Strive to get kids to open up by asking probing questions that require them to use as much language as possible. However, make sure you ask questions that are not too personal at first. I always joke with teachers that you do not want your students to be in the fetal position within the first three minutes you meet them. Keep in mind that you need to ease into a relationship before you get too detailed. Would you go on a first date and tell a person everything about yourself? You wouldn't if you wanted a future with that person. The same is true with getting to know your student. Aim for a positive experience—you want students to get excited about reading!

It's also important to remember not to make any assumptions. I once watched a volunteer ask a boy what his parents did for a living, and the child broke down in tears. Evidently, the boy's parents were both incarcerated, and he lived with foster parents. A less intrusive way to ask a question would be, "Who do you live with?" Once the child provides the details, then you can probe further. Keep in mind that this is the twenty-first century, and there are lots of different types of families. Some kids have no mommies, some have two mommies, and others have foster mommies. There are lots of different family structures, and we have to be respectful, conscious, and sensitive to each student's background.

What you really want to know is what turns this student on. Take a moment and jot down some questions that you can ask your student to try to get to know him or her:

1. _____
2. _____
3. _____
4. _____
5. _____

Like everything else in this book, I promise not to leave you hanging. If you get to your first session and freeze when it comes to asking your student questions, I have prepared a list of possible questions you can ask (see page 136).

"What if" questions are some of my favorites. I always try to prepare teachers and volunteers for the worst-case scenario. For example, if you ask a student what kind of pet he has, and the child starts crying and gagging, screaming, "I don't have a pet. Everyone else has a pet. WAAAA!" Don't panic. Take a negative and turn it into a positive.

"If you could have any pet in the world, what kind of pet would you have?"

After a thoughtful pause in his tantrum, the child pensively states, "Penguin."

This is a typical answer for a young child, and it still reveals exactly what you need. It tells you something about the student's interests. The better you get to know your students, the better you can help your students find their passion for reading. Before they find their passion for reading, though, you have to find their passion so you know what to offer them to read.

So—you've gotten to know your student a little bit. That is an essential step in designing an optimal reading fitness program. Now you have to show your student some of the equipment that is available to match his or her interests. Before you ever start reading with your student, it is important that you allow your student to choose something he or she would like to read. Chapter 8 covers introducing students to reading equipment to ensure they will become excited about their first reading session with you.

CHAPTER

BLOCK 2: BOOK TALK

All the best stories in the world are but one story in reality—the story of escape. It is the only thing which interests us all and at all times, how to escape.

ARTHUR CHRISTOPHER BENSON

When you go to a movie, do you write a report afterward that discusses the plot, characters, and theme? No—you talk about the movie with your friends. That's the same strategy you need to use when promoting good books: Lead book talks.

That's what Oprah does. All I ask out of life is for Oprah to read this book and mention on her show how much she enjoyed it. Do you know why? Whenever she does that, a book becomes an instant bestseller. Book talks are like commercials. Once you grab people's attention with subjects they are interested in, they are excited to know more about that subject. Do you remember how, way back when, after CBS showed a made-for-TV movie (for example, about astronauts), the star of the movie would always appear afterward and say, "If you enjoyed this presentation, here is a list of book recommendations about the subject that you can find at your local public library." I miss those teachable moments on television.

Book talks pump kids up about reading and show them what great materials are available. The first time I went to my local gym, the various machines and equipment overwhelmed me. Once a trainer took me on a tour and explained how various machines operated, however, I had a better idea of which ones matched my needs and interests. Parents and teachers can help students better understand the great stories that are available by exposing students to those stories. Since there are thousands of great stories available, students are sure to find something that they will enjoy.

There are a couple of elements to remember when leading a book talk. First of all, your objective is to interest students in reading something you promote. This is important because you want to be as familiar as possible with whatever book you choose to read together. Don't fall into the trap of reading with a student some book that you know nothing about, or you may encounter more than you bargained for (for example, profane language or disturbing situations). By carefully screening books before introducing them to your student, you can feel comfortable with whatever your student chooses. There are plenty of book summaries and reviews available online, or you could simply ask friends, teachers, or children's librarians for suggestions.

Pitch the books as if you were a used car salesmen highlighting a going-out-of-business sale. Clear your shelves and get the kids reading. You want students to share good books with you and with one another. By talking about books, you are utilizing the most tested, convincing, and effective form of advertising around: word of mouth.

Whenever I lead book talks, I make sure to include a variety of different titles. I like to make sure that the books relate to the interests of students. For example, when working with a single student as a reading volunteer, I like to highlight at least ten different reading materials during my first session with him or her. They don't have to all be books, as many students prefer comics, magazines, and newspapers. Generally, the vast majority of the titles I offer are books— that's just my preference, and I encourage you to choose for yourself. Everyone has his or her own tastes and preferences. Just make sure to provide students with variety so they can to choose something that they are interested in reading.

Where do you get books? Well, your home library is a good start. The classroom and school libraries are other options. There is also this government institution that provides free books for everyone's use. It's called the public library, and most communities have one—unless local governments have had to cut their funding to make room for important civic projects, like stadiums.

A lot of reading volunteers, parents, and teachers will ask me how they will know which books to showcase for students. My advice is to promote books that you have read and enjoyed yourself, as students will hear the passion in your voice and want to see what all the fuss is about. If you cannot think of anything, another good person to ask is a children's reference librarian. These folks literally have brains oozing out of their heads, they have read so many titles. By the way, reading lots of good books is the secret to a long life (along with a glass of red wine and a good walk every day). If you want to live longer and happier, turn off the TV and pick up a good children's book.

A TYPICAL BOOK TALK

I like to lead a book talk once a week and vary the titles. You should feel free to do the same. Again, I strongly suggest that you read books before you promote them, just in case the content is not what you may have thought. Reading books you are not familiar with can lead to dire results. For example, one volunteer that I trained had heard that *Goosebumps* books were very popular with kids, so she gave one to a first grader she was working with. The child had nightmares for weeks after being read aloud a particular story by her mother. Moral: Don't judge a book by its cover. You do not want your students to require therapy for years after they have had you. (Incidentally, *Goosebumps* books are fantastic interest-grabbers for fourth and fifth graders.)

Remember, this book is geared for those working with K–8 students, so the titles I model in this sample book talk relate to that age group. Still, keep in mind that variety is the spice of life, and just because a child is in first grade doesn't mean you should just suggest first-grade level books. For the sake of allowing the child to read on his or her own, though, make sure the bulk of your recommendations are for that reading level, and save the tougher texts for your read alouds.

Okay, ready for a book talk? Sit back and enjoy this sales presentation. (You can find a list of recommended books on pages 137-138.)

The first book I selected is *Anansi the Spider* (McDermott 1987). I chose this book because it has a medal on it so it must be good. Actually, it is not just any medal. It is the Caldecott Medal, which is awarded every year by the American Library Association (ALA) to the best children's illustrated book of the year, as voted on by children's librarians across the country. Every year they choose a winner and honor a few other titles, and these books are recommended anywhere in the country. For young adult books, the ALA presents the Newbery Award, which follows the same voting process. These books are the gold standard, and keep in mind that just because a book won an award does not mean you or your student will enjoy the book. Again, prescreen anything you introduce, or ask a children's librarian for advice.

Now, if you ever want to become a millionaire writing children's books, I recommend you put a medal on the cover, as that usually impresses the casual buyer. One person that heeded that advice was Sue Denim, who wrote a book called *The Dumb Bunnies* (1998), a hilarious parody of Margaret Wise Brown's *Goodnight Moon* (1947). There is a medal on the cover, and if you look closely it reads: "This book is too dumb to win an award." I enjoy this book because it is silly and funny. You may recognize the illustrator, Dav Pilkey, who is now a pretty big hit with kids around the country enamored with his Captain Underpants series.

The next book I'll suggest is *There's a Nightmare in My Closet* (Mayer 1992). I love this book because it is funny and deals with an issue many children deal with: being afraid of the dark. Children experience all sorts of problems and issues growing up. Whatever the problem, there is a children's book written about it, and this is a great way to deal with issues in a roundabout manner. There are children's books about manners, bullies, bed wetting, September 11—anything. Mercer Mayer, the book's author, also wrote the popular Little Critter series.

No discussion of children's literature can take place without promoting books by Dr. Seuss. There's a reason he is *doctor* and not mister. Dr. Seuss may be single-handedly responsible for teaching the world how to read in English (at least, before *Sesame Street* and a certain boy wizard). That dozens of publishers rejected his first book *And to Think That I Saw It on Mulberry Street* (1989) is beyond me; then again, tons of publishers showed J. K. Rowling the door, as well. Dr. Seuss is magical for many reasons. First, his books usually rhyme. Predictable rhyming patterns are essential for young and second language learners. He also likes to make up words in his stories, which is a great model for students to see how to play with language and have fun with words. (Edward Lear was one of the first masters of nonsense books.)

Dr. Seuss's books deal with a wide range of important issues, from protecting the environment to warning children about the dangers of nuclear war. He's pretty deep. And there's one area, in particular, that I think he is a genius for thinking about: He consciously drew his characters to be orange and purple and green so that they would be accessible to all children. Too many children's books feature nothing but white kids, and that leads me to my next recommendation.

I enjoy books by authors like Eve Bunting and Vera Williams because they are multicultural without usually being about culture. They simply make sure that character illustrations, names, and experiences represent an array of American experiences. Books do not have to be specifically cultural in order to demonstrate diversity. I have read a lot of books featuring Mexican American characters, and most of them have to do with tamales. If every book about white kids had to do with hot dogs, I'd gag! Culture goes beyond food. The United States is composed of people from all races, religions, and cultures. Our job as teachers is to ensure that diverse literature is represented in the classroom. It can be as simple as ensuring that books have pictures of children from different backgrounds and have names that students are or are not familiar with. Let's get beyond Dick and Jane and include Jose, Shaneka, Li, and Mohammed. Books are our passports to seeing the world. If you cannot find books that do this, use sticky notes and allow students to cover up character names with the names of fellow students and friends. Students can also re-illustrate pictures so that characters reflect diverse backgrounds. Finally, if you have students who all come from a similar background, keep in mind that while it is important to have books that reflect your students' experiences, it is even more important that teachers share books about people from different cultures. African American students need to be exposed to great Asian authors as well as great African American authors, and vice versa.

Biographies are vital for students to hear—it's important for them to see that they control their own destinies. Their choices shape their lives. Rhoda Blumberg's *Bloomers!* (1993) is a wonderful book about the first women to wear pants. *A Weed Is a Flower* (Aliki 1988) talks about the hard yet amazing life of George Washington Carver. If you have a student who enjoys soccer, find books about soccer players. There are always books that talk about how famous people started out. Even adults can benefit from these books; I admit I didn't know much about Jackie Robinson, but after reading *Jackie Robinson and the Story of All Black Baseball* (O'Connor 1989), a forty-eight-page children's biography of his life, I became intrigued to read more adult-level biographies about this fascinating historical figure.

Include books that have plenty of pictures of rocks, dinosaurs, insects, and animals. Younger children especially love animals. A great entry into the world of reading is to find wonderful picture books that give information about children's interests. Children may open picture books because they want to see the images, but the books work the same as TV with closed captioning—children are bound to notice the words eventually.

Find books that are different shapes and styles. There are Big Books, little books, hardcovers, paperbacks, pop-ups, and Leap Frogs. Many students become interested in books just because of their shapes. I have seen little kids who love finding the biggest book in the library, and I have witnessed older kids keep pocket-size books so they can read when they are bored or waiting in lines. My own students have marveled at books about crabs (and shaped like crabs), small books about small people (like *Harold and the Purple Crayon* [Johnson 1981]) and interactive books that talk to the reader (like Leap Frogs).

A terrible fact about schools is that most of them evaluate children based on their reading ability and then label the child's overall intellect based on that ability. Here's the problem with that scenario: A lot of my lowest readers have turned out to be my best mathematicians. Schools label poor readers as "behind," though, simply because their reading skills lag. A good way to interest our young mathematicians in reading is to provide math-oriented stories such as *One Grain of Rice* (Demi 1997), *Sir Cumference and the First Round Table* (Newschwander 1997) and *The King's Commissioners* (Friedman 1995). Author Greg Tang is one of my favorite authors who writes funny, intriguing books filled with math poetry.

Just about every child on the planet knows who *Sesame Street's* Grover is, and that is why I suggest *The Monster at the End of This Book* (Stone 2003). Children love reading about characters they are already familiar with. Remember your favorite book growing up? I enjoyed books such as *Curious George* (Rey and Rey 2001) because I was so enamored with the main character the same way children are drawn to Harry Potter (Rowling 1998) today.

How Do Dinosaurs Say Good Night? (Yolen 2000) is funny, but the book's biggest draw is that it shows lots of dinosaurs. Children love dinosaurs. I repeat: Children love dinosaurs! I once worked with a little three-year-old preschooler named Francisco. When I asked Francisco to say his name, he would struggle and say "Fran . . . Fwan . . . Fwan . . . ." But when I showed Francisco this book, he pointed excitedly and yelled "Tyrannosaurus rex!" Children simply love dinosaurs. Use them in your book talks.

Another one of my favorites is *Why the Sun and the Moon Live in the Sky* (Dayrell 1990). I love exposing students to folktales and legends. It is a great way to get students thinking about how to creatively explain how things come to be. After reading folktales and legends to my elementary students, I was surprised how much the students wanted to write their own legends. At one elementary school, the bell rang all the time. My students decided to create a ghost story/legend about an old principal who haunted the school by ringing the bell all the time. Another one of my classes once wrote a story that explained why the moon isn't always full—because it's hungry. Legends and folktales provide great stimulation for students to write, as well.

The Invisible Hunters/Los Cazadores Invisibles (Rohmer, Chow, and Vidaure 1993) is worth its weight in gold because it is written in two languages. More dual language books need to be published, and they will as more second language learners fill our classrooms. These books are great because they reinforce English and the students' native languages. Better still, many students' parents who may not be proficient in English can read the stories aloud in their native language to their children. Since the books are also written in English, many parents have commented how helpful these books are to their own English development, as well as their children's.

I encourage teachers to find books that children can act out. For example, with a ghost story—such as those in *More Scary Stories for Sleep-Overs* (Pearce 1992)—I always turn off the lights and tell the story with a flashlight held below my chin to add an eerie feeling. You can also shine the flashlight down on your face for romance stories. When I read books about nature, I ask students to read outside. Books about friends should be read by friends. Show children a variety of ways to make reading fun.

The True Story of the Three Little Pigs (Scieszka 1996) and stories like that are great fun for students who are familiar with old tales and nursery rhymes and enjoy hearing alternate versions of the story. These stories are usually great for giggles and getting students to constantly think about different points of view and how they can rewrite stories. One teacher, in fact, always asks students to think of sequels to their favorite stories or to draw a cover based on the story that would make other students want to pick up that book.

Find books about the communities your students live in. When I was working with eighth graders in the Watts area of Los Angeles, I used books by Walter Mosley (for example, *Always Outnumbered, Always Outgunned*, 1998) because he is from Watts and writes about that area. My students could relate to it. Eve Bunting's books (for example, *Your Move*, 1998) about Los Angeles were great motivators, too. If you can't find students books specifically about where you live, find books about your region or state or lifestyle.

Nursery rhymes, fables, and myths, of course, are also very important. A great way to get parents into the classroom is to ask if there are different versions in different cultures.

Predictable pattern books like *I Went Walking* (S. Williams 1996) are great for repeated readings and increasing students' confidence in reading.

Poems are great for those students who don't want to read an entire book. Shel Silverstein (*Where the Sidewalk Ends*, 2004) is particularly popular with kids. According to the American Library Association, his books are stolen more than any other author's from public libraries, so he must be pretty popular. Another one of my favorite authors of funny children's poetry is Jack Prelutsky (*It's Raining Pigs and Noodles*, 2000).

There are classics that I feel children need to be exposed to, like *Winnie the Pooh* (Milne 2001), *Where the Wild Things Are* (Sendak 1988), *Madeline* (Bemelmans 1958), and *The Berenstain Bears* (Berenstain and Berenstain 1983). Again, by talking about books that you read and treasured as a child, you are able to pique the interests of your students. Another trick here is to specifically give a book to a student and say, "I enjoyed this and I know you enjoy motorbikes, so I picked this out for you because I knew you'd like to read about the motorbikes in this story." In my experience, when students are given books in this manner, they almost always make an attempt to read them at the very least.

Finally, *Tuesday* (Wiesner 1991) is a Caldecott Winner, but more importantly it is a book with fewer than twenty vocabulary words. It is filled with bizarre and beautiful illustrations that ensure incredibly detailed descriptions from students. A great habit to get students into is to tell stories in their own words; picture books are just the trick as a precursor to more conventional reading.

So, after hearing about all of those books, have I convinced you to read at least one of them? A book talk is a great way to get kids motivated to read. So many students just need recommendations from trusted sources like teachers, parents, and volunteers.

Now that you have aroused the interest of your student to read, it is important to build that student's confidence in reading. Picture reads are designed to help students become familiar with a story before they are faced with reading the story. There is always a great book for a picture read, which leads us to the next block in the Six Blocks program.

DISCUSSING BOOKS IS IMPORTANT

When people see movies or hear songs or eat at restaurants that they really enjoy, they want to tell people about them. The same is true for books. Discussing books is one of the greatest rewards of reading, as it allows readers an opportunity to compare their interpretations of what they have read. It is important for teachers to discuss books with students and allow students to discuss books with one another (Allington 1994; Manning and Manning 1984). Especially with younger students, discussing books allows more time for students to enhance their language skills (Worthy 1996).

Elementary teachers do not need to devote a large amount of time to book discussions, but they should allow discussions to flow freely. What is important for teachers to understand is that students should be allowed to discuss books freely rather than to be forced to perform traditional book reports (Manning and Manning 1984). Young children, just as older children, need an opportunity to express their excitement or dismay at what they have read (Palmer, Codling, and Gambrell 1994). In addition, Manning and Manning (1984) show that students who read stories and then discuss them with their teacher and classmates perform better on tests of reading growth and attitude than those who read without discussion. By providing students with the time to talk about books, teachers are sending an important signal to students: Books are an important way of sharing knowledge and relating pleasurable experiences with one another.

HIGH INTEREST BOOKS ARE IMPORTANT

Without high-interest, quality reading materials, many students will remain unaffected by increased exposure to books. Access to books means very little if the books provided hold little interest to the students served. Students need to be permitted to choose the materials they wish to read. For example, flooding an elementary classroom with a thousand new books has little to offer students if none of the books have pictures or stories that students would find interesting. To increase the number of reading materials without ensuring high-interest literature is like providing starving people canned foods without a can opener: The gesture is nice, but fails to accomplish its purpose. It is necessary to provide students who are hungry to read with interesting reading materials they can open.

Worthy (1996) has found that many students do not have reading materials at home that interest them. As a result, schools play an important role in providing high-interest materials. Unfortunately, most classrooms do not offer the types of books students are curious about reading (Allington 1994). This is a mistake, as many librarians agree that one of the single greatest ways to improve students' reading habits is by allowing them to read books that interest them (Worthy 1996). While many may argue that allowing students to read materials that interest them impedes their exposure to more so-called academic literature, research (Krashen 2004) indicates the contrary: Increased exposure to high-interest reading materials—often considered to be light reading—helps students develop the skills to read more complicated, academic-oriented texts. Next time you catch a student reading a copy of People magazine, keep in mind that he or she student is well on the way to enjoying Macbeth.

CHAPTER

BLOCK 3: PICTURE READ

A picture is worth a thousand words.

NAPOLEON BONAPARTE

If a picture is worth a thousand words, why not use that to your advantage as a reading teacher? Just because a student cannot read the words of a story does not mean they have to miss out on the story. The beauty of a good picture book is that no matter who you are, you can look at pictures and tell a story. This is a useful technique for a number of reasons. First, parents with limited reading skills have a way to spend time reading with their students, making this a great strategy to suggest at parent conferences—everyone can look at pictures. Additionally, glancing through the pictures gives us a good idea of what the story is about and makes the text more comprehensible. Finally, emphasizing oral language development is always a good idea, because it is a precursor to better reading development.

After you have spent some time talking to your student about his or her life and recommending a variety of fun books to read, I recommend leading a picture read. This activity is designed to enhance students' oral skills while directing their attention to books. Before you ever open a book, take the opportunity to ask the student questions about the book. By directing the student's attention to pictures and words in the title, you can help the student make predictions about the book's content. (See page 139 for samples of the types of prediction questions you can ask students.)

Next, explain to your student that there are different types of reading. For example, computers read numbers; we read environmental print every day, like street signs and billboards. Inform your student that for this portion of your reading session, you will read the pictures in the book. You will not read a single word, but you will try to figure out what the story is about based on the pictures. Make sure to guide the student along, and, if the student does not immediately describe important story information in particular pictures, direct the student's attention to that information. Ask leading questions like so many telemarketers, pollsters, and yellow journalists have perfected (Would you like to make more money? Would you like to spend more time with your family? Would you like to know about an amazing opportunity that will only cost you nineteen dollars a month for eternity?). You can get anyone to say anything if you ask a question in the right way. The purpose of this exercise is to help students develop a context for the story before they read a single word.

Have you ever seen a movie that was based on a book? It is easier to understand the movie if the story is already familiar to you. Picture reading allows students to become familiar with stories without worrying about reading the words. You can still read the actual words during your read-aloud time or even allow the student to read the story on his or her own after you finish the picture read. Like all of the strategies listed in this book, a picture read is meant to be a fun, confidence-building activity that students will employ on their own inside and outside of school.

As you guide your student through a picture read, consider the following steps.

> 1. Take a look at the cover. Tell your student what the title of the book is and who the author and illustrator are. Try to make

your student familiar with terms like *title, author,* and *illustrator* and what each means. Ask your student to tell you what he or she sees in the picture on the cover. Ask a number of leading questions to help the student try to predict what the story is about. (See page 139 for sample leading/predicting questions.) Tell your student that you are going to read all of the pictures in the book like archaeologists and try to determine what the book is about with out any words.

2. As you turn each page and examine each picture, ask your student what is happening in the picture and what each picture might tell about the story. Constantly ask your student leading questions and allow your student to make predictions about what is going to happen next.

3. Ask your student what he or she thinks about the story. Is this an easy story to figure out from the pictures? Does your student like the story so far? Point out that it is all right to select a different book if this book does not hold interest. There are plenty of good books out there, so don't waste time on a book that your student is not interested in. Always remember to keep the picture read fun.

4. You may picture read the entire story, but experience has taught me that it is often preferable to stop reading about three pages before the story ends. Again, allow your student to predict the story's ending and see if he or she is right. This is a good way to keep up interest and build curiosity about how the story ends.

5. Ask your student if he or she would like to read the story with words, offering a variety of options: be read aloud to; read aloud; partner read the story; read the story silently alone; or read the book in some other way.

Keep in mind that there are all sorts of ways to conduct the picture read activity; these are only a few suggestions based on strategies that teachers have told me have worked best with their reading volunteers. Picture reading is a vital, developmentally appropriate step for teachers to encourage their students to use in developing their awareness about print. It's meant as a fun activity and a way to get students to discuss elements of the books they are reading. I enjoy using picture reads with students because they make great segues for the next block in the Six Blocks program—reading aloud to students.

CHAPTER 10

BLOCK 4: READ ALOUD

Every time we read to a child, we're sending a "pleasure" message to the child's brain. You could even call it a commercial, conditioning the child to associate books and print with pleasure.

JIM TRELEASE

In the early 1980s, a panel of researchers issued the seminal report entitled *Becoming a Nation of Readers*, which reported that the single greatest activity you can do to help your child's reading is to read aloud. If that is the case—and I believe it is—the single greatest resource you can use to help you with reading aloud to your students is Trelease's *Read-Aloud Handbook* (2001). This is the one book (besides this one, of course) that I recommend for all teachers, parents, and administrators to purchase. It is worth its weight in gold.

The first half of the book reviews the research that proves why reading aloud is the most valuable activity you can do with your students. The second half of the book summarizes all sorts of books for all sorts of elementary age levels that are excellent for read alouds, and also details specific strategies for reading aloud. To quote Trelease, "If reading aloud cost $129, we'd have it in half the homes in America, and if the kids hated it, we'd have it in every classroom" (2001, 14). I agree. A lot of folks avoid it simply because it is such a simple activity. They should refer to medieval philosopher William of Occam who gave us Occam's Razor, which states that one should not increase, beyond what is necessary, the number of entities required to explain anything. Put another way: Keep it simple, silly!

While I promised not to bombard you with academic research, I would like to emphasize how vital reading aloud is to the success of getting students to read for fun. A number of studies conducted around the world champion reading aloud to children (Elley 1989; Feitelson, Kita, and Goldstein 1986; Heath 1983; Morrow 1991; Ricketts 1982). Exposure to books through read alouds has long been considered one of the primary factors in developing students' vocabulary, comprehension, fluency, and writing (Krashen 1985; Senechal 1997). In addition, research has shown that reading aloud to children is closely related to improving students' motivation to read on their own (Brassell 2003; Routman 1994). Reading aloud to students allows them not only to listen to the sounds and rhythms of language but also provides students with positive feelings about books. It's the first step toward familiarizing students with books and getting them excited about reading.

Research has shown that most children who cannot read in first grade remain unable to read in the fourth grade. Reading aloud to children, therefore, is critical to students' early schooling—it clearly makes a difference to their later schooling. For example, Hall (1987) found a significant relationship between seven-year-olds' reading test scores and concepts about print and the amount of read alouds they encountered. Other studies support these findings, as reading aloud has been found to heavily influence students' vocabulary knowledge (Elley 1989; Lambert 1991; Robbins and Ehri 1994). Elley (1980, 1989) examined the second language vocabulary acquisition of children who listened to stories and found rapid growth in English language development for children with greater amounts of free reading exposure, leading him to conclude that stories read aloud with brief explanations offer a great resource for vocabulary acquisition. Lambert (1991) replicated Elley's (1989) study and found that second language learners who listened to stories in English showed similar gains in second language vocabulary acquisition, specifically when the reading of the text was scaffolded for the child to facilitate understanding.

When children repeatedly interact with stories they learn a great deal of vocabulary and syntax (Elley 1991; Senechal 1997) in addition to demonstrating increased comprehension (Dennis and Walter 1995). Learning is facilitated by the story context and subsequent mediation that may function as the scaffold necessary for such learning to take place. Finally, reading aloud has been found to significantly contribute to the lifelong appreciation for books and reading; people who read more perform better in reading. Reading aloud, therefore, is a vital part of children's literacy development.

READ ALOUD GUIDELINES

Now that I have bombarded you with a bunch of academic research proving reading aloud's worth, following are a few simple suggestions for teachers, parents, and volunteers who read aloud to students.

Preread

It is important that you read any book to yourself before you read it aloud to your student. You never know how a story may turn out, and you want to make sure the story is appropriate for students. If you are unsure, you can always ask a children's librarian. Another trick is to select books that you really like, as your student will surely sense your passion and enthusiasm for books. The more you get into a book, the more likely your student will become interested in a book.

Rome Wasn't Built in a Day

At first, it is better to read shorter passages to students. Listening is a learned skill developed over time. Be patient, and anticipate that your student, especially a younger child, will not sit still long for stories. Over time, your student will manage to sit for longer periods. A lot has to do with the way you present stories and pictures, too.

Welcome Comments

You are not in a movie theatre or a church with one hundred people. It is all right to allow your student to shout out observations, comments, and questions. Try to encourage him or her to interact with the story. Feel free to stop on any page and allow your student to comment on pictures, make predictions, and ask questions. The more reading aloud is a shared activity, the more excited your student will become. I love to select books for read alouds that are highly interactive. Good interactive books are those where students get to make noises or repeat phrases or make movements.

Replay the Hits

Children love to hear good stories over and over again. The more times they hear a story, the more confident they become at telling the story themselves. Allow your student to read aloud stories to you, too. Again, the more you involve a student with a read aloud, the better he or she becomes at reading the story.

Keep It Cozy

Sit close to your student when you read so he or she can see the pictures in the book. Don't insist that your student sit in a hard chair or in any manner that feels uncomfortable. Reading aloud should be a sensory experience that promotes positive tastes, feelings, sounds, sights, and smells.

Have Fun!

Reading aloud should be as much fun for you as it is for your student. The better the read aloud, the better the impact on your student. I have seen teachers destroy totally cool books with dull readings. I have also witnessed teachers liven up boring books with different character voices and lots of gestures. Make your presentation memorable.

No matter what you have planned for your Six Blocks program, I insist that you schedule some time to read aloud. Reading aloud is the most effective way to get students reading. If you don't believe me, grab a copy of Trelease's book (2001). Reading aloud is vital to a student's reading improvement, and it is doubly useful when paired with partner reading—the next block in the Six Blocks program.

READING ALOUD IS ESSENTIAL

While providing students with increased access to books is a pivotal and necessary step in motivating students to read, it is also clearly not a sufficient measure in promoting greater literacy skills. Beyond access to books, one of the most important first steps in encouraging students to read is for teachers or parents to read stories with their children (Trelease 2001; Yaden, Smolkin, and Conlon 1989).

Reading aloud to children costs nothing, takes only a minor amount of time, and provides both reader and child with precious interaction revolving around books. It is considered by many researchers to be the most important activity in developing a child's literacy (Routman 1994; Wells 1986). In fact, the Commission on Reading, created by the National Academy of Education and the National Institute of Education and funded under the U.S. Department of Education, stated in its report Becoming a Nation of Readers that "the single most important activity for building by knowledge required for eventual success in reading is reading aloud to children" (Anderson, Hiebert, Scott, and Wilkinson 1985, 23). Therefore, the most important thing teachers need to know is that reading to students greatly enhances students' reading ability, reading attitude, and language acquisition.

If the goal of many schools is to provide students with the literacy activities they may not be receiving at home, reading aloud to students is an important, cheap, and easy activity that can have long-term benefits for students. Especially for low-socioeconomic status (SES) students, reading aloud to preschoolers tends to make the start of elementary school easier on them (Bus, van Ijzendoorn, and Pellegrini 1995).

According to research conducted by DeBarshye (1993), reading to students may be the most important at a very young age. Young students who are read to read more on their own and show greater interest in reading (Morrow and Weinstein 1982, 1986). Of all the studies conducted by researchers on the benefits of storybook reading with and to children, however, look no further than Trelease 2001:

We read to children for all the same reasons [we] talk with children: to reassure, to entertain, to inform or explain, to arouse curiosity, to inspire. But in reading aloud, [we] also condition the child to associate reading with pleasure, create background knowledge for the child and provide a reading role model. (2001, 6)

CHAPTER

BLOCK 5: PARTNER READ

The path to greatness is along with others.

BALTASAR GRACION, SPANISH PRIEST

This next block in the Six Blocks program comes with a warning: Partner reading can be a little scary. It may not work the first time. And it may not work the second time. But remember, if at first you don't succeed, try, try again. Partner reading is sort of like dancing with a new partner: It takes a couple of tryouts before you stop walking on each other's feet. Think of this portion of your reading fitness regimen as lifting weights for the first time. After the first couple of workouts, you may leave feeling sore, but it gets easier and benefits you immensely in the long run.

What is partner reading, anyway?

In education we like to give programs and strategies unique names like *Six Blocks*. The problem is everyone wants to give a strategy his or her own name, even if the same strategy has been used fifty trillion times previously. For example, reading for fun is referred to as free voluntary reading (FVR), drop everything and read (DEAR), sustained silent reading (SSR), uninterrupted sustained silent reading (USSR), and any other acronym you can imagine. I have heard all sorts of different names for partner reading, but an easy way for teachers to remember it is to think of it as stereo reading. Partner reading is simply the teacher and student reading the same page aloud at the same time. This, along with reading aloud, is an activity that I really encourage teachers to use every session they spend with their student. My past trainees have universally praised it as one of the most important keys to the Six Blocks program.

So how do you partner read? First, select a book. It can be the book you used for the picture read or the read aloud, or it can be a new book. It always depends on the student. Some students prefer to use the same book for all three activities, as the reinforcement builds their confidence with a certain book. Researcher Tim Rasinski [1990] at Kent State has written all sorts of wonderful articles and books that emphasize the importance of repeated readings. It is up to you and your student. After the first couple of meetings, however, I suggest you allow the student to choose. After all, the more choices students are allowed to make, the more empowered they feel.

Make sure you select an easy book to read for your first session. Your goal should be to hear your student say, "This is easy!" You are trying to build students' reading confidence, and gradually advancing the complexity of text is a great way to improve their reading ability.

For the first couple of partner reads, it is important that you, the teacher, point to the words as the two of you read. While your student may want to point to the words—and will get the chance to later—it is really important that you model this behavior first. It is advisable that you use your finger to point, not a pencil—I have seen plenty of students who would later not read a book simply because they did not have a pencil!

Attitude is everything. You have to get the student excited, so make a big fuss. "Are you ready to have fun partner reading? I love partner reading! We get to read in stereo. Are you ready?"

To synchronize your reading, come up with a countdown with your student. There are all sorts of options: 3-2-1, apples-bananas-oranges, tres-dos-uno, Kobe-Shaq-Phil, whatever excites your student. Once you have your countdown, announce it together, and you, the teacher, point to the words as you begin to read.

Whenever I show teachers and volunteers how to partner read with students, I role-play as the teacher and a volunteer trainee plays the student. What I have found is that the volunteer trainee does a great job in her role as a student reader. So we reverse roles, and I allow the volunteer trainee to play the teacher while I play the student reader.

Instead of us saying together "Once upon a time," it goes more like this:

TEACHER: Once
STUDENT: nce . . .
TEACHER: upon—
STUDENT: pon . . .

The student is always a little bit behind the teacher because she is waiting for the teacher to read the words. This is typical for students who are struggling readers. If they are synchronized, it's even better, but I always prefer to prepare teachers for tough scenarios.

Keep in mind that there is nothing wrong with the student being a little behind. In fact, expect the student to be a little behind. This is a great opportunity for you to take an informal assessment of the students' reading fluency. If the student is not keeping up, try to slow down. If the student is still having a difficult time not keeping up, you should recognize that the student is having a difficult time decoding and recognizing words, to say nothing of comprehending the story. In that respect, I have come across students who are able to recite like a robot "Once . . . u . . . pon . . . a . . . time . . . there . . . were . . . three . . . bears." When you ask them what is going on in the story, they respond in an equally monotone voice: "I . . . have . . . no . . . i . . . de . . . a." So keep in mind that while you are paying attention to students' fluency, asking questions about the story is a good way to check their comprehension. Again, this assessment is simply to help you when selecting books with your student. It is not meant as a way to judge his or her ability but should be used as a way to design activities that will better assist them.

During your first few partner reads together, you will probably want to do a countdown before you read each new page, as your first couple of sessions may be a little bumpy. Once you get used to each other, however, you will only have to do the countdown when you begin a book. You'll get to know each other's habits like an old married couple.

Now, I suggested earlier that the teacher point to the words. Isn't that going to drive students nuts? Yes. So, if they want to start pointing to the words, they are going to have to give you a signal. I usually ask students to signal by tapping me on the shoulder. If you are one of those people who declares, "I don't want any children touching me!"—fine. Have the student tap on the table or desk. The important thing is that you and the student establish a signal that signifies for you to stop partner reading in stereo. Your student wants to do a solo.

After the student gives you the signal, stop pointing to the words *and* stop reading aloud. The student is now reading aloud on his or her own *and* pointing to the words on his or her own. You are just an observer and cheerleader.

The teacher/volunteer's role in partner reading is like that of a weightlifting partner. Whenever you lift weights you should have a partner to spot you. A good spotter simply ensures that if you start to struggle lifting a specific weight, you do not have to fear dropping the weight on yourself. Your spotter is there to give you extra assistance. Following is an example of what to do—how to be a good spotter— when a student struggles on a particular word.

Your student tries to read the sentence, "We'd like some electric blankets" (from *Click, Clack, Moo* [Cronin and Lewin 2000]). The student has no problems reading the first part of the sentence: "We'd ... like ... some . . . ." But then all of a sudden, the student is stuck.

What are you going to do?

Many teachers'/volunteers' first reaction is to tell the student the word *electric*, but is that a good strategy? What will the student do when you are not around? Keep in mind that you are trying to breed an independent reader.

Here's a tip: Do you have a significant other? How about an insignificant other? When you get in an argument, before you say something you might regret, what are you supposed to do? Count: one, one thousand . . . two, one thousand . . . three, one thousand . . . four, one thousand . . . five, one thousand. I want you to count to five and give your student a chance to get the word. Many times they'll get the word, if you just give them a chance. For some reason Americans are so darn impatient. We want everything immediately. Maybe we'd mellow out if we had to stand in bread lines or toilet paper lines for hours on end.

Here's another bit of advice. Make sure to count to five in your head, or else you're just going to add more pressure. We don't want the student sucking his or her thumb or getting into the fetal position, do we?

While you are waiting for your student to figure out the word, pay attention to what he or she is doing. Is he or she sounding out the word? Looking at the picture? Looking at the ceiling? Whenever you see a child looking at the ceiling, that's known as the prayer strategy, when the student looks to the heavens and asks, "Oh Lord, please tell me this word." That only works for the most faithful and sin-free students.

After giving the child a chance to say the word, don't give the student the answer. Instead, train the student to use different strategies to figure out what the word is. Strategies include sounding out the word. Not a bad idea, although I suggest attacking the word in chunks rather than phonetically sounding out each letter. Why? English is not a phonetic language! Spanish is. If you look at *a* in Spanish, it always sounds like *ahh*. In English, *a* can sound like that, as in *awesome* and *autumn*. It is also featured in words like *hay* and *say*. It *can make many handsome and unattractive* sounds. English is just a mess to try to understand phonetically. That's why you can phonetically spell *fish* as *ghos*. The *gh* makes the /f/ sound as in *enough*; the *o* makes the /i/ sound as in *women*; and the *s* makes the /sh/ sound as in *sugar*. Do you see why a lot of students are not so hooked on phonics?

The nice thing about English is that its blends make fairly consistent sounds, like the /th/ blend. *That there* is *the* best *thing* I've heard. *Thanks. Then* you go to the store to buy ingredients and find parsley right beside the *thyme*. Isn't English a pain? Do you now have a little bit more empathy for students trying to learn English as a second language? Imagine what a child who is having difficulties reading must feel when faced with so many rules. The fact is, there are too many to remember, and they often contradict one another. That is just one of the reasons that it is highly improbable that most children learn English in a segmented way.

Sure, there are other suggestions you can give the student that may prove to be helpful. Look at the word like a dirty garage, and don't try to attack it all at once. Rather, focus on parts before examining the whole. You can also give clues such as: What sound does the word start or end with? What does the word rhyme with?

If the picture reveals a word, direct the student's attention to the picture. For example, if there is a picture of a *black* cat, and the student gets stuck on the word *black*, suggest that he or she look at the picture. "Starts with what sound? B? And look at the picture . . . is that a blue cat? No? It's a black cat. Good."

Another strategy is to do something that good readers like you practice every day: skip the word. When you are driving on the road and come across a pothole, you don't slam on the brakes, do you? If you do, I'll make sure to report you to the Department of Motor Vehicles . . . how about I report all people who drive and talk on cell phones while I'm at it? You don't stop and get out a road guide to determine what to do when encountering a pothole. You drive around it or over it. When you come across words that you don't know while reading the daily newspaper, you don't stop, get up, and say "I'll go get my dictionary and determine what the word means." You skip over the word and try to determine its meaning from context. Nine times out of ten you will either figure out the word or realize that understanding that particular word is not vital to understanding the story. What's more important, understanding every word or comprehending the overall message? Politicians would have a rough time if we held all readers to that standard.

I do not mean to suggest that you should give all of these clues to the student. I simply want you to have these and other strategies up your sleeve. Please don't use all of them on one word, though. The longer the student stays stuck on the word, the more you can see the perspiration forming on his forehead, his face brightening to an unlovely red, and his hands shaking. Always remember to keep reading fun, and if it looks like the student is just not going to get the word, simply tap him on the shoulder (or tap the table, for those of you who fear physical contact with little people). Redo your countdown, resume pointing to the word in question, and begin to partner read in stereo again until the child taps you. In this way, you read the word together. You did not give away the word to the student.

As you can see, partner reading is not exactly the world's easiest process, but trust me: The more you practice, the better the two of you will get.

I am often asked, "What if the kid never taps you?" This is an outstanding question. What book are you going to partner read for your next session together? The same book. But what if the kid doesn't tap you that time? What book are you reading the following session? The same book. Experience has shown me that by the fourth reading, most students will want to read aloud on their own to impress you.

They may not be reading the words. They may have memorized them. That's what a lot of children do. They understand that the symbols are what you read, not the story's picture, but they can't quite grasp what this is all about. That's fine. That's an important print concept they've mastered, and they are well on their way to conventional reading skills. In the meantime, repeated readings should help build their confidence. If they don't, chances are you picked out a book that is too difficult and should find something a bit easier. That's why I stress that you begin with something very easy. If you don't know what books are easy, check them out for yourself or ask a children's librarian.

You may have noticed that this activity may not be the quickest activity in the world, and that is fine, too. If you have to cut into another block in your Six Blocks program, do it. You can always shuffle blocks and reprioritize them from week to week. I offer six blocks so that you are overprepared to work with your student. Try not to ever take more than two blocks of time, however, on any single activity. Most people have short attention . . . what was I talking about? Oh, yes. Most people have short attention spans.

I hope you can see the benefits of partner reading. I feel it is an important confidence builder for many students. It is a great way to share books and stimulate conversations. It also leads to a variety of games and writing activities, as discussed in Chapter 12.

PROVIDING STUDENTS WITH READING OPPORTUNITIES IS IMPORTANT

Increasing the amount of books makes little difference if students are not provided with a chance to read the books—a point worth emphasizing for those developing educational policies. Beginning in daycare centers and continuing throughout secondary school, students should be allowed many opportunities to read on their own. Partner reading builds the confidence in students to attempt reading books on their own.

In studies of reluctant readers, Worthy (1996) determined that while access is indeed one of the central issues in determining students' attitudes toward reading and whether they choose to read voluntarily; she also identified two other important issues: choice and opportunity. Each of these factors, in addition to greater access to books, is important in the literacy development of a child.

Trelease (1995) says that "the lack of sustained silent reading time and the continued reliance upon worksheets to improve reading skills is like the drunk looking for his keys under the streetlight: he knows he didn't lose them there, but the light is better" (p. 16). While drill-and-kill activities such as worksheets have failed to significantly increase standardized reading test scores, many teachers rely on worksheets because they are "easier." Programs designed to provide students with time to read for themselves, meanwhile, have fallen by the wayside.

The importance of allowing students time to read cannot be over-stated. Anderson (1996) found that the number of minutes younger students are allowed to read each day is an important predictor of their future reading achievement. The findings of Cunningham and Stanovich (1998) support this premise. If students do not spend much time reading at home, then it is the responsibility of schools to provide students with time to read. Neuman's observations (1999) of students in hundreds of early literacy programs confirmed that more reading is generated by students when they are allowed free choice time to do so. So why don't schools allow students greater opportunities to read? If you do not want to partner read with your student, at least allow time for your students to select a book to read on their own. It makes a difference!

CHAPTER

BLOCK 6: WRITING AND GAMES

If there's a book you really want to read, but it hasn't been written yet, then you must write it.

TONI MORRISON

All right, so now that you've done all this reading, grab a pencil and paper and write about the book's plot, theme, and main characters. Maybe you could fill out a worksheet that summarizes the story. Sounds like fun, right?

Remember these words: Book reports suck. Book reports are one of the traditional tasks that get students to hate reading. What do you do after you see a good movie? I'll tell you what you don't do—you don't write a critical review. So why do we ask children to do the same thing after reading a good book? How can we turn writing into a fun activity rather than a punishment? Traditional book reports successfully offend students' interest in reading and writing.

I observed one first-grade teacher who always stops reading stories three pages before the end of the story. She turns to the kids and tells them to write the ending. In this way, her students have to use their imaginations and come up with thoughtful conclusions. It is also a great comprehension exercise to see if the kids have been following the story. Sometimes the kids come up with endings that are better than the actual story endings.

A kindergarten teacher cannot ask her students to write because most have just learned letters in the alphabet. One teacher I know has students create story murals that capture the story in pictures. Another asks students to design book covers. In much the same way that movie posters give patrons hints at a story's plot points, so too do students' book covers. When I taught preschoolers, I simply asked students to dictate what they remembered from the story, and I would create a class Big Book that the students could illustrate themselves.

God's gift to teachers is the 99-cent discount store. One teacher I've observed buys a bunch of journals at the 99-cent store every year and distributes them to each of her students. She encourages students to write their thoughts and questions in the journals, and then she responds. Since she began her 99-cent store literacy project, she has seen a dramatic increase in the number of journals she receives every night, as students are anxious to see what their teacher is going to write in them. I have also seen teachers give students journals so that they can write to one another, and one teacher's third graders particularly enjoy alternating sentences to create their own silly stories in their journals.

Creating comics strips is always a hoot. Cause and effect drawings, as well as sequence of events, are good activities to take students through. I watched a fourth-grade teacher who used to be an actor liven up his discussions with students by acting like different characters and encouraging his students to do the same. Every time he reads a good story, he acts like a big Hollywood mogul and says, "Kids, this book is great. You gotta write me the sequel!" Students scribble stories like *Little Red Riding Hood 2: The Wolf's Revenge*, and *Humpty Dumpty Sits on a Chair!*

You can ask your students to write reviews about their likes and dislikes and have them paste feedback on the back cover ("the best book I have read in years" or "a nonstop thrill ride"). You can write letters back and forth, or you can even encourage your student to write letters to authors or submit letters to newspapers; many newspapers have children's pages that accept student ideas, anecdotes, jokes, and riddles. I spoke with a fifth-grade teacher who had a wonderful idea for her students to do at home: Email authors reviews of their books. She was amazed that not only did most authors respond to her students, but most of her students began reading and writing more as a result. Online bookstores like amazon.com also boast great areas for students to write reviews of books they have read.

The point is that writing does not have to be a drag. Song lyrics and poems are great ways to get kids motivated to write. If you are working with an outgoing thespian student, she should relish the challenge to write her own roles and produce plays for her class. Writing should always be a fun activity that students will want to do outside of school. That's why I know games are so powerful to student learning.

To quote the wise teacher Mary Poppins, "For every task to be done, there is an element of fun." Translated, that means that games are good. Repeat: Games are good. Humans are naturally drawn to things that give them pleasure. The power of games is that students will do them in their free time again and again, so the more ways you can get students to make reading and writing fun, the better.

One of my favorite writing games with students is *Mad Libs*. *Mad Libs* take two people—one person asks a partner to give the name of a proper noun, an active verb, the name of a food, an adverb ending in -ly, and so on. You don't need another person, but it is a lot more fun to have another person—you want to be able to share your story afterward for laughs. The partner writes your responses in blank spaces in a prewritten paragraph and reads the new silly story. You can get *Mad Libs* at any bookstore, find free ones on the Internet, or create your own.

Check most daily newspapers and you are bound to find a variety of word games. Crosswords, word finds, and word jumbles are just a few of the wonderful activities that can draw your student to reading and writing. Once your student picks up the habit of playing these games, it is difficult to give them up. The more enjoyment your student finds from these activities, the more likely he or she is to pursue these games for a lifetime. In the process, you are also encouraging her to read the newspaper daily.

Board games may sound ancient in the computer age, but they are still excellent motivators for students. They are especially important to students who may not have computers at home because board games do not cost a lot of money. In fact, good teachers can support classroom activities where students create their own copies of games to take home, such as drawing pictures and words on small index cards and matching the correct pairs to make a fun Concentration memory game. Good teachers are problem solvers—do not allow lack of funding to prevent you from using a variety of games in your classroom. I created more than thirty games for my first class simply by using items such as cardboard boxes, milk cartons, and index cards.

I save writing and games for the last block of the Six Blocks program session because I want them to serve as an incentive for students to finish their other reading activities. Teachers, parents, and volunteers always ask me what incentives are appropriate to reward students for their reading efforts. Candy, soda, and cash may be popular with students, but these types of external rewards do not lead to reading interest. Children are a lot brighter than we give them credit for. They know that if adults have to bribe them to do something, the activity is not worth doing on its own. While I am grateful when people experiment with ways to encourage students to read more often, I question if rewards are the best message to send students.

I was fortunate to be broke when I began my teaching career because I was never tempted to buy students pizza or supply them with candy bars. I did not have the money to buy those types of rewards, so I implemented cheaper solutions. First, I rewarded students with reading time. By emphasizing the importance of reading as a reward, I wanted students to understand that reading was a fun reward after a hard day's work. I would also reward students by reading an extra story aloud to the class (for example, turning out the lights and reading a ghost story with a flashlight), allowing students to write silly songs that they could perform, or letting students read aloud to younger students in other classrooms.

More than any other reward, praising students is highly underrated. When teachers give students specific praise on their activities, students take pride in their work. All students are anxious to please their teacher or parents, even if they don't show it. Simple words of encouragement can have a powerful impact on a student's behavior, and I highly recommend using praise as an effective, inexpensive reward with your students.

Remember to be specific, though, as general praise comes across as flattery. For instance, you could say, "Thanks for showing up on time, Cynthia." Or you could say, "I am always so glad to see you in your seat, Cynthia, because you are always on time with a smile on your face, and you are always ready to help others. I am grateful you are here. Please don't ever change."

Which compliment would you prefer?

If you insist on providing your student with external rewards for reading, how about taking your student to a bookstore to watch an author speak or visiting locations from a story. I used to take my own students to Olvera Street in Los Angeles because it is prominently featured in a story I always read with them. Why not hand out bookmarks, pencils, journals, and books as prizes? Children value whatever they perceive you, the teacher, value. When I was growing up, one teacher offered "the prestigious penny" to the student who finished with the highest grade in each academic subject. Students battled to win the prize. It was only a penny, but since the teacher placed value on it, students decided it was worth having.

The final block in the Six Blocks program is to reward students for their progress in reading by encouraging fun writing activities and other games. Some teachers use this time to talk with students about their progress, and that is great, too. Use the time to show students that their efforts are appreciated. Your opinion matters.

CHAPTER

TIME TO TAKE ACTION

To add a library to a house is to give that house a soul.

CICERO

It seems logical: We become better readers by reading (Goodman 1982; Smith 1988). Unfortunately, reading for fun is not the priority of most schools. It is nobody's fault, as the pressure to improve students' reading achievement has led some teachers, parents, and administrators to sacrifice any fun activity in school for the sake of raising students' test scores. That's why many elementary schools fail to provide adequate time for art, music, and physical education. Field trips and school libraries have been cut from budgets to allow for more test preparation materials. As concerned adults have modified their curricular reading programs to boost test scores, they have inadvertently created a generation of students who view reading as a mechanical, highly directed, and boring task. Rather than pointing fingers over past errors, let's focus on solutions to remedy the situation.

Books make a difference: We should *celebrate* reading rather than *prepare* for it.

I have never encountered a parent, teacher, administrator, or volunteer who questions the need for books in our school libraries and classrooms. However, I have had to defend the importance of making proper time and space for books. While most schools see the importance of books, too many—especially in many so-called underachieving areas—fail to provide an adequate supply of books. A limited variety of books in terms of interest, topic, language, reading level, and structure lessens the effectiveness of most school reading programs.

An abundance of research exists that emphasizes the importance of increased access to books for students. Access to books is a necessary, though not sufficient, component of a child's literacy development. Increased exposure to books improves reading ability, reading attitude, and language acquisition. While making books available to students is crucial, other considerations must be made in preschool and elementary school literacy programs. Teachers must model reading behaviors to their students, such as reading aloud to their students and reading for pleasure when students read for pleasure. Enabling students to choose books that specifically interest them allows students to enter the wonderful world of imagination spurred by books, while book discussions help bring stories to life for students. Finally, a quality school reading program allows students time to read on their own.

In my many years of training people, I have marveled at the successes of teachers, parents, administrators, and volunteers utilizing the Six Blocks program for simply an hour a week over a six-month period. In many cases students improved their reading test scores, but that statistic fails to capture the imagination. What gets me excited about Six Blocks is its universal impact on developing struggling and reluctant readers into passionate and avid readers. Students who used to hate or fear reading because of their negative experiences now cannot wait to confidently talk about the books, magazines, and newspapers they have read.

As a teacher, you have chosen to make a difference. Ten years from now, your past students are not going to remember you for *what* you taught them or *how* you taught them. Your past students will only remember *how you made them feel*. I thank you for taking the time to

TIME TO TAKE ACTION

try out Six Blocks with a student or to train a parent, administrator, or volunteer to use Six Blocks with your students. On your journey, please feel free to share any questions, comments, or anecdotes with me via my website at www.lazyreaders.com. Good luck!

APPENDIX

QUESTIONS, ANSWERS AND CHECKLISTS

One who asks a question is a fool for five minutes; one who does not ask a question remains a fool forever.

CHINESE PROVERB

This section answers some of the oft-repeated questions that teachers, administrators, reading volunteers, and parents ask at my trainings. It is by no means definitive, and I try to provide succinct answers. Additionally, I provide a number of checklists that you may use when undertaking the Six Blocks program with your students.

I view reading the way I view going to the gym: I know it's good for me, but I don't enjoy it. How do I help a student enjoy reading?

I can relate, as I spent most of my childhood despising books and ignoring the gym. The problem was that I did not surround myself with peers and role models who made reading or exercise fun for me. Our job as volunteers and educators is to find the particular interests of our child and design a program around that child's interest. Football coaches got me to exercise because I enjoyed football as a child, and one reading teacher in particular got me interested in books by allowing me to choose books for myself. Every child is different, so try to let the child's interest influence how you make reading fun for that child.

How do I get a child to read if he or she shows no interest in books?

Books have a lot of competition nowadays among video games, television, movies, the Internet, and so on. I think students tend to steer away from books because they think of reading as assigned reading. Let's be clear: It is only reading when you choose to do it for yourself. Forcing children to read will produce the same results as forcing them to exercise: They will resent you and the activity. Determine students' interests and build on those. Develop a reading fitness plan that is unique to each particular child. Just like there are a variety of tools designed to enhance upper body strength (bench press, rowing machines, dumbbells), there are a variety of materials that may assist reluctant readers (comic books, scripts, brochures, magazines, short chapter books). The more you can get a student to read anything, the greater that student's chances are to successfully read books.

What if I do not have an hour to work with my student? Will Six Blocks still work?

Certainly! The key to teaching is flexibility, and I always emphasize to volunteers and teachers that my suggestions are just that: Suggestions. Many people spend more than ten minutes on specific activities, while others eliminate activities that they or their students do not enjoy. Many ESL pull-out teachers that I have worked with only get thirty minutes a week with their students, and I have advised them to either shorten the blocks to five minutes each or to work on half the blocks every other week. Use whatever works for you.

How can I adapt Six Blocks when I have so many standards to teach and tests to administer?

I realize that teachers have a lot of content to cover and standards to accomplish. What I see lost in the process is student motivation and enjoyment of reading. My goal in presenting these ideas to you is to show you how to make reading a fun habit that students can turn to in an age where schools often sacrifice learning for teaching. When I say that, I mean that too many teachers are pressured to teach a zillion content and test items. While students may learn the information necessary to pass tests, very little sticks with them because it is not meaningful or interesting to them. I have found that Six Blocks reestablishes reading as a fun habit rather than a chore.

What if I come across a situation with a student that I do not know how to handle?

I often encounter individuals at trainings that nod throughout my presentation and find they have a zillion questions after working with their student for the first time. Feel free to contact me through my website, www.lazyreaders.com, if you ever have any questions or would like to share some successful strategies that have worked for you.

BLOCK 1:
QUESTIONS YOU CAN ASK STUDENTS AT YOUR FIRST MEETING

Often, teachers and volunteers get stumped on what to ask students. My advice is to avoid "yes" or "no" questions. Here are some suggested questions:

- What's your favorite _____ (anything—subject in school, pro sports team, book, hobby, and so on)?
- Who do you live with? (Important: Be sure to ask the question this way, and remember not to make any assumptions about students' backgrounds. There are lots of different family structures, and it seems to work best to find out the structure first and then follow up with other questions.)
- How did you learn to read?
- What do you like most about school?
- What do you like to do when you are not in school?
- How can I make reading fun for you?
- Who is your idol?
- What books do you own at home?
- Where would you go if you could go anywhere?
- Where is your favorite place to read?
- How often do you go to the public library? Bookstores?
- When do you like to read?
- How do you like reading?
- If you could go anywhere, where would you go?
- If you could be anybody, who would you be? Why?
- What would you do on your perfect day?

APPENDIX

BLOCK 2: BOOK TALK

This list of recommended books represents the books that I discuss in Chapter 8.

Aliki. 1988. *A Weed Is a Flower: The Life of George Washington Carver*. New York: Aladdin.
Bemelmans, Ludwig. 1958. *Madeline*. New York: Viking Juvenile.
Berenstain, Stan, and Jan Berenstain. 1983. *The Berenstain Bears and the Truth*. New York: Random House Books for Young Readers.
Blumberg, Rhoda. 1993. *Bloomers!* New York: Antheneum.
Brown, Margaret Wise. 1947. *Goodnight Moon*. New York: HarperTrophy.
Bunting, Eve. 1998. *Your Move*. New York: Harcourt Children's Books.
Dayrell, Elphinstone. 1990. *Why the Sun and the Moon Live in the Sky*. Boston: Houghton Mifflin.
Demi. 1997. *One Grain of Rice*: A Mathematical Folktale. New York: Scholastic Press.
Denim, Sue. 1998. *The Dumb Bunnies*. New York: Blue Sky Press.
Friedman, Aileen. 1995. *The King's Commissioners*. New York: Scholastic.
Johnson, Crockett. 1981. *Harold and the Purple Crayon* (50th Anniversary Edition). New York: HarperTrophy.
Mayer, Mercer. 1992. *There's a Nightmare in My Closet*. New York: Puffin.
McDermott, Gerald. 1987. *Anansi the Spider: A Tale from the Ashanti*. New York: Henry Holt & Co.
Milne, A. A. 2001. *The Complete Tales and Poems of Winnie the Pooh* (75th Anniversary Edition). New York: Dutton Juvenile.
Mosley, Walter. 1998. *Always Outnumbered, Always Outgunned*. New York: Washington Square Press.

Newschwander, Cindy. 1997. *Sir Cumference and the First Round Table*: A Math Adventure. Boston: Charlesbridge.

O'Connor, Jim. 1989. *Jackie Robinson and the Story of All Black Baseball*. New York: Random House Books for Young Readers.

Pearce, Q. L. 1992. *More Scary Stories for Sleep-Overs*. Los Angeles, CA: Price Stern Sloan.

Pilkey, Dave. 2002. *The New Captain Underpants Collection: Box Set* (Books 1–5). New York: Blue Sky Press.

Prelutsky, Jack. 2000. *It's Raining Pigs and Noodles*. New York: Greenwillow.

Rey, Margaret, and H. A. Rey, 2001. *The Complete Adventures of Curious George* (60th Anniversary Edition). Boston: Houghton Mifflin.

Rohmer, Harriet, O. Chow, and M. Vidaure. 1993. *The Invisible Hunters/Los Cazadores Invisibles: A Legend from the Miskito Indians of Nicaragua*. San Francisco: Children's Book Press.

Rowling, J. K. 1998. *Harry Potter and the Sorcerer's Stone*. New York: Arthur A. Levine.

Scieszka, Jon. 1996. *The True Story of the Three Little Pigs*. New York: Puffin.

Sendak, Maurice. 1988. *Where the Wild Things Are* (40th Anniversary Edition). New York: HarperCollins.

Seuss, Dr. 1989. *And to Think That I Saw It on Mulberry Street*. New York: Random House Books for Young Readers.

Silverstein, Shel. 2004. *Where the Sidewalk Ends* (30th Anniversary Edition). New York: HarperCollins.

Stone, Jon. 2003. *The Monster at the End of This Book*. New York: Golden Books.

Tang, Greg. 2001. *The Grapes of Math*. New York: Scholastic Press.

Wiesner, David. 1991. *Tuesday*. New York: Clarion.

Williams, Sue. 1996. *I Went Walking*. Sydney: Red Wagon Books.

Williams, Vera B. 1991. *Cherries and Cherry Pits*. New York: Greenwillow.

Yolen, Jane. 2000. *How Do Dinosaurs Say Good Night?* New York: Blue Sky Press.

APPENDIX

BLOCK 3: PICTURE READ

Before meeting with students, select a book to picture read and have some questions ready to ask your student before opening the book:

1. What do you see in the picture on the cover?
2. What is the title of the book?
3. Who is the book about?
4. What do you think the book is about?
5. Why do you think the book is about that?
6. What do you think is going to happen in this book?

Before reading the story, tell your student to keep some questions in mind while reading the story. By doing this, your student will have a purpose for reading the text. Of course, you can review these questions during and after the story. Sample questions include:

1. Who is the main character in the story?
2. Where does the story take place?
3. What would you do if you were in the main character's shoes?
4. Why do you think the main character acts the way she does?
5. How could you make the ending different?
6. Why do you think the story ends the way it does?

One final tip: Encourage your student to ask questions, too. Asking questions generates and builds interest and assists in comprehension and fluency.

BLOCK 4:
READ ALOUD

There are three components to reading aloud: selecting a good book, the read aloud itself, and previewing/reviewing the read aloud. The best resource to assist you is Trelease's Read-Aloud Handbook (2001). Here are a few of my suggestions:

1. Select a Good Read-Aloud Book
- Know the interests of the child: Talk with the child and get to know him or her better.
- Choose "just right" topics and text. Try to find books that 0.27 in discuss timely topics and measure the difficulty level of the text. Remember, you can FEAST on three books a day with your student by providing variety: Favorite books, Easy books and Tough books.
- Use books focused on the child's needs.
- Help the child gain appreciation of literature. The key is variety, variety, variety.
- Incorporate books of poetry and songs.
- Choose readable nonfiction.
- Remember the child's favorite authors.
- Repeat readings of old favorites.
- Choose easy books that the student can read on his or her own.
- Choose tough books that the student cannot read on his or her own.

2. The Read Aloud
Use questions to
- create connections,
- generate predictions, and
- elicit possible solutions.

Use stopping points to
- ask for predictions,
- elicit connections—ask how the child sees his or her own experiences reflected in the story and how he or she sees similarities between this story and other stories,
- cue children to join in the refrain or pattern,
- clarify an unusual word or concept, and
- check for understanding.

3. *Preview and Review the Book*

Introducing the book
- provides an overview of the book,
- allows the child to make predictions by looking at the cover,
- taps the student's prior knowledge of the topic, genre, and author, and
- highlights potentially difficult concepts or words.

Use questions before the story to
- determine prior knowledge about topic, setting, and genre, and
- help the child create connections.

Use questions after the story to
- generate connections, and
- evaluate predictions and solutions.

Some general tips for reading aloud with your student include:
- Always make time to read aloud.
- Read in a cozy place.
- Read anything the child likes.
- Select several books at a time for read alouds.
- Read and sing.
- Select books with colorful pictures.

- Involve the child—allow the child to echo read, make sound effects, and so on.
- Read a book you create together.
- Hold a prop (puppets, stuffed animals) while reading.
- Read predictable stories.
- Have a plan but be flexible.
- Read with emotion and keep your presentation lively.
- Use stopping points, or quick spot checks, to keep children engaged, especially "wiggly" students.
- Speak slowly and clearly and make eye contact whenever possible.
- Always provide a variety of books, formats, and experiences.

APPENDIX

BLOCK 5: PARTNER READ

Here is a quick guide to keep in mind when performing a partner read with your student:

1. Select an easy book; increase difficulty each session with the student.
2. Make a positive comment about reading with the child, for example, "I am so excited to read with you today, Gonzalo!"
3. Point to the words as you read. When the student gets better, allow him or her to point to words.
4. Create a countdown (3-2-1, apples-bananas-oranges) to synchronize reading with your student.
5. Read aloud together in sync.
6. When a student wants to read aloud on his own, have him or her signal you by tapping you on the shoulder or tapping the desk.
7. Stop pointing to words and reading aloud; instead, allow the student to read aloud on his or her own.
8. If a student comes to a word he or she has difficulty with, count to five and allow the child to try to determine the word on his or her own.
9. After five seconds, if the student still has not correctly produced the word, give clues such as:
   - What sound does the first letter make?
   - What does this word rhyme with or sound like?
   - Look at the picture.
   - Use word chunks; break down the word into smaller parts.
   - Skip the word and try to determine meaning based on context.
10. If the student cannot produce word after receiving clues, tap the student on the shoulder. Redo the countdown,

point to the word, and read the word together.

Keep in mind that partner reading takes a little time to perfect, so you and your student may struggle a bit at first. However, experience has shown me that students and volunteers usually develop good rhythm to the activity after a few attempts. Students and volunteers often remark how enjoyable and beneficial the activity is.

APPENDIX

BLOCK 6: WRITING AND GAMES

Writing can be a drag for many students because they associate writing with book reports and essays. By exposing students to different writing activities and games, we can increase students' interest in writing. Here is a list of writing activities and games that I have found to attract students' interest and motivation in writing.

1. *Concept of Word*: Write words on cards. Give to student. Student recites her word in an oral sentence or writes a sentence with word.
2. *Name Bags*: Place letters of child's name in a bag. Have child put letters in order (can later be done with others' names).
3. *Show Me*: Fold paper three times, and fold up bottom to create pockets. Student spells three-letter words (e.g., C-V-C).
4. *Treasure Hunts*: Use word and picture cards to guide student to prizes (e.g., bookmarks, pencils, and so on) you have hidden.
5. *Silly Poems*: Help student create poems with pretend words, à la Lewis Carroll's Jabberwocky.
6. *Word Hunts*: Have student search in newspapers for words that begin with certain letters, and so on.
7. *Spice It Up*: Student spices up newspaper articles by creating better words for said, says, and so on.
8. *Word Family Bingo*: Practice word family endings (-at, -an, and so on).
9. *Guess That Word*: Think of a common sight word and give student clues to guess the secret word. Student writes down her guess after each clue is given (e.g., "Write": five letters, starts with a /w/ sound, something you do every day, and so on).

10. *Journaling*: Ask student to keep journal with reactions about reading. Parents can do this, too.
11. *Give a Story/Get a Story*: Tell a descriptive story to student and ask student to write you a story that reminds her of your story.
12. *Write the Headline*: Show student a photo from a newspaper or magazine and ask student to write a headline or caption for the photo.
13. *Which Word Fits*: Ask student to complete sentence with different words ("Find a word that starts with *f* and fits into this sentence: 'I like to play with my _____.'").
14. *Hollywood Writer*: A few pages before you finish a read aloud, ask student to write the ending.
15. *Hollywood Movie Star*: Ask student to make obscure characters more prominent in the story.
16. *Hollywood Producer*: Ask student to write a sequel to a story he enjoys.
17. *Hollywood Publicist*: Don't show the pictures or the book cover, and ask student to design the cover based on the story after you've read it together.

Additionally, encourage students to make lists, create maps, share recipes with instructions, play board games, write funny stories, and so on. The point is to make writing a fun activity where students are engaged and learn to understand the usefulness of writing.

APPENDIX

SIX BLOCKS: READING SESSION AND ORGANIZATIONAL STRUCTURE

1. TALK: *(10 minutes)* Get to know your student.	2. BOOK TALK: *(10 minutes)*	3. PICTURE READ: *(10 minutes)* Set up content.
4. READ ALOUD: *(10 minutes)*	5. PARTNER READING: *(10 minutes)*	6. WRITING AND GAMES: *(10 minutes)*

Each box represents ten minutes of your session.

Focus on developing an appropriate pace and the preferred activities as you get to know your student. You will find that some activities may take much longer than ten minutes, or you may decide to shuffle the activities in a different order (for example, paired reading may take twenty minutes or a student may prefer to journal at the beginning of the session). Do not worry about having to conform to the time or the structure. This plan is simply a starting point.

©2018 by Danny Brassell from *The Reading Breakthrough*.
For more info, go to: www.ReadBETTERin67Steps.com.

SIX BLOCKS

Date:_____ Student: _____

1. TALK *(10 minutes)*	**2. BOOK TALK** *(10 minutes)*
3. PICTURE READ *(10 minutes)*	**4. READ ALOUD** *(10 minutes)*
5. PARTNER READING *(10 minutes)*	**6. WRITING AND GAMES** *(10 minutes)*

Comments: _____
_____
_____
_____

©2018 by Danny Brassell from *The Reading Breakthrough*.
For more info, go to: www.ReadBETTERin67Steps.com.

REFERENCES

Allington, R. 1994. "The Schools We Have. The Schools We Need." *The Reading Teacher*, 48: 14–29.

Allington, R. L., and P. M. Cunningham. 1996. *Schools That Work: Where All Children Read and Write.* New York: HarperCollins College.

Anderson, R. C. 1996. "Research Foundations to Support Wide Reading." In *Promoting Reading in Developing Countries*, edited by V. Greaney. Newark, DE: International Reading Association.

Anderson, R. C., E. H. Hiebert, J. A. Scott, and I. A. G. Wilkinson. 1985. *Becoming a Nation of Readers.* Washington, DC: U.S. Department of Education, The National Institute of Education.

Anderson, R. C., P. T. Wilson, and L. G. Fielding. 1988. "Growth in Reading and How Children Spend Their Time Outside of School." *Reading Research Quarterly*, 23: 285–303.

Barclay, K., C. Benelli, and A. Curtis. 1995. "Literacy Begins at Birth: What Caregivers Can Learn from Parents of Children Who Read Early." *Young Children*, 50 (4): 24–28.

Brassell, D. 1998. "Maestro, Can We Go to the Library Today? The Role of the School Library in the Improvement of Reading Attitudes and Achievement Among Bilingual Elementary Students." In *Literacy, Access, and Libraries Among the Language Minority Population*, edited by R. Constantino. Lanham, MD: Scarecrow Press.

———. 1999. "Creating a Culturally-Sensitive Classroom Library." *The Reading Teacher*, 52 (6): 651–652.

———. 2003. "Celebrity Readers." *Knowledge Quest*, 32 (2): 50–51.

Bus, A. G., M. H. van Ijzendoorn, and A. D. Pellegrini. 1995. "Joint Book Reading Makes for Success in Learning to Read: A Meta-Analysis of Intergenerational Transmission of Literacy." *Review of Educational Research*, 65 (1): 1–21.

Constantino, R. 1995. "Two Small Girls, One Big Disparity." *The Reading Teacher, 48* (6): 504–505.

Cronin, D., & Lewin, B. 2000. Click, Clack, Moo: Cows That Type. New York: Simon & Schuster Children's Publishing.

Cummins, J. 1991. "The Role of Primary Language Development in Promoting Educational Success for Language Minority Students." In *California State Department of Education, Schooling and Language Minority Students: A Theoretical Framework*. Los Angeles: Evaluation, Dissemination and Assessment Center, California State University.

Cunningham, A. E., and K. E. Stanovich. 1998. "What Reading Does for the Mind." *American Educator* (Spring/Summer): 8–15.

DeBarshye, B. D. 1993. "Joint Picture-Book Reading Correlates of Early Oral Language Skill." *Journal of Child Language, 20*: 455–461.

Dennis, G., and E. Walter. 1995. "The Effects of Repeated Read-Alouds on Story Comprehension as Assessed Through Story Retellings." *Reading Improvement, 32* (3): 140–153.

Dupuy, B., and J. McQuillan. 1997. "A Touch of . . . Class!" *The Canadian Modern Language Review, 53* (4): 743–745.

Elley, W. B. 1980. "A Comparison of Content-Interest and Structuralist Reading Programs in Nuie Primary Schools. *New Zealand Journal of Educational Studies, 15*: 30–55.

———. 1984. "Exploring the Reading Difficulties of Second Language Learners in Fiji." In *Reading in a Second Language*, edited by J. C. Alderson and A. Urquart. New York: Longman.

———. 1989. "Vocabulary Acquisition from Listening to Stories." *Reading Research Quarterly, 24* (2): 174–188.

———. 1991. "Acquiring Literacy in a Second Language: The Effect of Book-Based Programs." *Language Learning, 41* (3): 375–411.

———. 1992. *How in the World Do Students Read?* Hamburg: International Association for the Evaluation of Educational Achievement.

———. 1998. *Raising Literacy Levels in Third World Countries*: A Method That Works. Culver City, CA: Language Education Associates.

Farris, P., and M. Hancock. 1991. "The Role of Literature in Reading Achievement." *The Clearing House*, 65: 114–117.

Feitelson, D., B. Kita, and Z. Goldstein. 1986. *Effects of Reading Series Stories to First Graders on Their Comprehension of Language*. Haifa, Israel: University of Haifa, School of Education.

Gambrell, L. B. 1996. "Creating Classroom Cultures That Foster Reading Motivation." *The Reading Teacher*, 50 (1): 14–25.

Gaver, M. 1963. *Effectiveness of Centralized Library Service in Elementary Schools*. New Brunswick, NJ: Rutgers University Press.

Goodman, K. 1982. *Language and Literacy*. London: Routledge & Kegan Paul.

Greaney, V. 1996. *Promoting Reading in Developing Countries*. Newark, DE: International Reading Association.

Hall, N. 1987. *The Emergence of Literacy*. Portsmouth, NH: Heinemann.

Hayes, D. P., and M. Ahrens. 1988. "Vocabulary Simplification for Children: A Special Case of 'Motherese.'" *Journal of Child Language*, 15: 395–410.

Heath, S. B. 1983. *Ways with Words: Language, Life and Work in Communities and Classrooms*. New York: Cambridge University Press.

Houle, R., and C. Montmarquette. 1984. "An Empirical Analysis of Loans by School Libraries." *The Alberta Journal of Educational Research*, 30 (2): 104–114.

Krashen, S. D. 1985. *Inquiries and Insights: Second Language Teaching, Immersion, and Bilingual Education Literacy*. Hayward, CA: Alemany Press.

———. 1988. "Do We Learn to Read by Reading?: The Relationship Between Free Reading and Reading Ability." In *Linguistics in Context: Connecting Observation and Understanding*, edited by D. Tannen. Norwood, NJ: Ablex.

———. 1995. "Free Voluntary Reading: Linguistic and Affective Arguments and Some New Applications." In *Second Language Acquisition Theory and Practice*, edited by F. R. Eckman, et al. Mahwah, NJ: Lawrence Erlbaum Associates.

———. 1998. "Why Consider the Library and Books?" In *Literacy, Access, and Libraries Among the Language Minority Population*, edited by R. Constantino. Lanham, MD: Scarecrow Press.

———. 2004. *The Power of Reading* (2nd ed.). Englewood, CO: Libraries Unlimited.

Lambert, J. G. 1991. "The Effects of Oral Story Sharing on Vocabulary Acquisition in English as a Second Language Class." Unpublished manuscript. Los Angeles: University of Southern California.

Lance, K. C., L. Welborn, and C. Hamilton-Pennell. 1993. *The Impact of School Library Media Centers on Academic Achievement*. Castle Rock, CO: Hi Willow Research and Publishing.

Manning, G., and M. Manning. 1984. "What Models of Recreational Reading Make a Difference?" *Reading World, 23*: 375–380. McCracken, R. A., and M. J. McCracken. 1978. "Modeling Is the Key to Sustained Silent Reading." The Reading Teacher, *31*: 406–408.

McEvoy, G. F., and C. S. Vincent. 1980. "Who Reads and Why?" *Journal of Communication, 30*: 134–140.

Morrow, L. M. 1991. "Promoting Voluntary Reading." *Handbook of Research on Teaching the English Language Arts*, edited by J. Flood, J. M. Jensen, D. Lapp, and J. R. Squire. New York: Macmillan.

Morrow, L. M., and C. Weinstein. 1982. "Increasing Children's Use of Literature Through Use of Program and Physical Changes." *Elementary School Journal, 83*: 131–137.

———. 1986. "Encouraging Voluntary Reading: The Impact of a Literature Program on Children's Use of Library Centers." *Reading Research Quarterly, 21*: 330–346.

Nagy, W., P. Herman, and R. Anderson. 1985. "Learning Words from Context." *Reading Research Quarterly, 20*: 233–253.

Neuman, S. B. 1999. "Books Make a Difference: A Study of Access to Literacy." *Reading Research Quarterly, 34* (3): 286–311.

Palmer, B. M., R. M. Codling, and L. B. Gambrell. 1994. "In Their Own Words: What Elementary Students Have to Say About Motivation to Read." *The Reading Teacher, 48*: 176–178.

Powell, W. 1966. "Classroom Libraries: Their Frequency of Use." *Elementary English, 43*: 395–397.

Rasinski, T. V. 1990. "Effects of Repeated Reading and Listening While Reading on Reading Fluency." *Journal of Educational Research, 83* (3): 147–150.

Rasinski, T. V., and A. D. Fredericks. 1991. "The Akron Paired-Reading Project: Working with Parents." *The Reading Teacher, 44* (7): 514–515.

Rasinski, T. V., and N. D. Padak, 1998. *Effective Reading Strategies: Teaching Children Who Find Reading Difficult* (2nd ed.). Columbus OH: Merrill/Prentice Hall.

———. 2001. *From Phonics to Fluency: Effective Teaching of Decoding and Reading Fluency in the Elementary School*. New York: Longman.

Rasinski, T. V, N. Padak, W. Linek, and E. Sturtevant. 1994. "The Effects of Fluency Development Instruction on Urban Second Grade Readers." *Journal of Educational Research, 87*: 158–164.

Ricketts, J. 1982. "The Effects of Listening to Stories on Comprehension and Reading Achievement." *Direction, 18*: 29–36.

Robbins, C., and L. C. Ehri. 1994. "Reading Storybooks to Kindergartners Helps Them Learn New Vocabulary Words." *Journal of Educational Psychology, 86* (1): 54–64.

Routman, R. 1994. *Invitations: Changing as Teachers and Learners K–12*. Portsmouth, NH: Heinemann.

Senechal, M. 1997. "The Differential Effect of Storybook Reading on Preschoolers' Acquisition of Expressive and Receptive Vocabulary." *Journal of Child Language, 24* (1): 123–138.

Smith, F. 1988. *Joining the Literacy Club*: Further Essays into Education. Portsmouth, NH: Heinemann.

Snow, C. E. 1990. "Rationales for Native Language Instruction: Evidence from Research." In *Bilingual Education: Issues and Strategies*, edited by A. M. Padilla, H. H. Fairchild, and C. M. Valadez. Newbury Park, CA: Sage Publications.

Snow, C., M. S. Burns, and P. Griffin. 1998. *Preventing Reading Difficulties in Young Children.* Washington, DC: National Academy Press.

Stanovich, K. E. 1986. "Matthew Effects in Reading: Some Consequences of Individual Differences in the Acquisition of Literacy." *Reading Research Quarterly, 21*: 360–407.

Stanovich, K. E., and A. E. Cunningham. 1992. "Studying the Consequences of Literacy Within a Literate Society: The Cognitive Correlates of Print Exposure." *Memory & Cognition, 20*: 51–68.

Taylor, N. E., I. H. Blum, and D. M. Logsdon. 1986. "The Development of Written Language Awareness: Environmental Aspects and Program Characteristics." *Reading Research Quarterly, 21* (2): 132–149.

Tobin, A. W., and J. J. Pikulski. 1988. "A Longitudinal Study of the Reading Achievement of Early and Nonearly Readers Through Sixth Grade." In *Dialogues in Literacy Research: 37th Yearbook of the National Reading Conference Yearbook*, edited by J. Readance and R. Baldwin. Chicago: National Reading Conference.

Trelease, J. 1995. *The Read-Aloud Handbook* (4th ed.). New York: Penguin.

———. 2001. *The Read-Aloud Handbook* (5th ed.). New York: Penguin.

Von Sprecken, D., and S. Krashen. 1998. "Do Students Read During Sustained Silent Reading?" *California Reader, 32* (1): 11–13.

Wells, G. 1986. *The Meaning Makers: Children Learning Language and Using Language to Learn.* Portsmouth, NH: Heinemann.

Wheldall, K., and J. Entwhisle. 1988. "Back in the USSR: The Effect of Teacher Modeling of Silent Reading on Pupils' Reading Behavior in the Primary School Classroom." *Educational Psychology, 8*: 51–66.

Worthy, J. 1996. "Removing Barriers to Voluntary Reading for Reluctant Readers: The Role of School and Classroom Libraries." *Language Arts, 73*: 483–492.

Yaden, D. B., Jr., L. B. Smolkin, and A. Conlon. 1989. "Preschoolers' Questions About Pictures, Print Conventions, and Story Text During Home Read-Alouds." *Reading Research Quarterly, 24*: 188–214.

SPECIAL SNEAK PEEK OF

SECRETS OF SUCCESSFUL READERS

Engaging Comprehension Strategies for School & Home

DR. DANNY BRASSELL

America's Leading Reading Ambassador
and author of the Top-Selling Book
Bringing Joy Back into the Classroom

NIFTY WAYS TO ENGAGE STUDENTS' READING INTEREST

Remember: the more we can get students interested in reading, the more we can get them reading. The more they read, the better they will get at comprehending what they read. Here are some cool ways to engage students' reading interest…

> "Any book that helps a child to form a habit of reading, to make reading one of his deep and continuing needs, is good for him."
>
> –Maya Angelou

Reading Necklaces

I got this idea from watching the movie Dances with Wolves. Go to a handicraft store like a Michael's (or, you may be able to find this at some WalMarts) and purchase a bead kit. It should cost around $20. Give children plastic necklaces and every time they read for 20 minutes, they earn a bead to add to their plastic necklace. I'd wander around my classroom complimenting students on their beaded necklaces. "Oh, Shaneka, you have many beads," I'd say. "You are very wise."

Green Light: Go!

Go to an office supply store like Staples (or, as always, you may be able to find these at WalMart) and purchase green stickers, yellow stickers and red stickers. Every time a kid reads a book that he likes, he puts a green sticker on the inside cover, every time he reads a book that he thinks is so-so, he puts a yellow sticker on the inside cover and every time he reads a book that he does not like he puts a red sticker on the inside cover. For my class, when a book got five red stickers, we had a funeral for that book and donated it to the principal!

Australian Pete and Co.

When I was a teacher, as the days and months wore on, you could feel the energy drain from my students. On days when my students would fail to pay attention or lack energy, I'd complain to them that they weren't listening to a thing I was saying, so I was going to have to grab Australian Pete to read to them. I'd walk outside my classroom, come back in, tip my imaginary hat, grab my belt buckle as I straddled in and say, "G-day mates! I just got done puttin' a shrimp on the barbie. Your teacher asked me to read to you." And my students would cheer, "Yay, it's Australian Pete!" Just so you're clear, it was me.

In the late afternoon, I'd become "grumpy old man." I'd waddle in the room with my hunchback, waving an imaginary cane and an aggravated scowl, "You kids shut up! Your teacher wants me to read to ya." And the kids would cheer, "Yay! It's grumpy old man!" I should warn that one got me in trouble. One day a parent approached me and asked, "Did some mean old guy tell my kid to be quiet?" "Oh, I'll ask him not to come back." Yikes!

Campfire Interactive Reads

I sound more and more like an old guy every day. When I was a kid, kids knew some stuff. They could sing *God Bless America*. They knew their nursery rhymes. They had been to church and in Cub Scouts. Nowadays I see so many kids that literally know nothing. They need "playdates." Take them away from their electronic devices, and they appear helpless. When I was a kid, it could be 30 degrees below zero outside, but if I tried to set foot in my house after school my mom would shout, "Dinner's at six. Now go outside and play!"

Kids don't face boredom nowadays because they always have a device, whether it's a Smartphone or tablet. I call them "vidiots." They don't know what it's like to sit in a doctor's waiting room with nothing to do. They never think about looking out of the windows of their cars when they can watch a DVD in their minivan. And they certainly don't know how to create their own games.

When I was a Cub Scout, one of the games our den mothers taught us were campfire interactive reads. Before you read a story, give different characters, settings or places sound effects. For example, when I read *A Christmas Carol* to students, every time I read aloud Ebeneezer Scrooge, the kids all say, "Bah humbug!" Every time I say Bob Cratchett, the kids shake their heads and say, "Ahhh." And every time I say Tiny Tim, the kids put their hands together in prayer, nod their heads, smile and chime, "God bless us, everyone!" This is a great way to keep the kids engaged as I read the story, and besides – it makes me laugh. Make sure you're having fun when you're reading with your child.

California Jones

One of the games I created for my students is a game you can play with your child. I called it "California Jones," because I live in California, so you can name it after whatever state you live in. Here's how you play: you are a good-looking archaeologist who discovers amazing treasures every day. You just don't know what they are, so you have to tell us a story about them.

So let's say you hand your child a staple remover. The child with no imagination whatsoever will tell you a story about a staple remover. But we can do so much better than that! Encourage your child to be creative. What else could a staple remover be? Vampire teeth! A snake. If you're a middle school teacher, you'd automatically shout out "weapon!" To a middle school teacher, everything is a potential weapon. It can be a greater than/less than sign, a zit popper, an ear piercer, a shoelace de-tier, etc. Get the idea?

The Book Fairy

I have never been a fan of grading. There is no research to support a relationship between grades and what students learn. What there is research on is attendance. So Woody Allen was right when he said that 80 percent of success is showing up. One of my biggest priorities as a teacher was making sure my students showed up. Kids who don't miss school perform significantly better than those who do miss school. I was constantly seeking ways to entice my kids to come to school.

My second year teaching second grade I noticed that my lowest attended day of the week was Tuesday. I never understood why, but for some reason, more kids than normal missed school on Tuesdays. So I tried to think of a way to get the kids to show up, and I came up with "the book fairy." Before students would show up to class, I placed a book on each of their desks, and on each book I placed a Post-It note. The Post-It note would say something like, "Niceysha – here's a book about horses. I know how much you like horses. Love, The Book Fairy."

Niceysha would show up to class, see the book on her desk and yell, "The book fairy was here! The book fairy was here!" Once I started doing the book fairy, my attendance on Tuesdays shot up to almost 100 percent.

Read to a Stuffed Animal

I once had a student in my class named Isabel who had recently immigrated from Guatemala and did not speak much English. For two weeks I never heard her speak. So one day I gave her a Teddy bear and said, "Isabel, this Teddy bear doesn't know how to read. Can you teach him how to read?" And ten minutes later I heard Isabel's voice for the first time. Granted, the book I gave her was in English, and she was reading it aloud in Spanish. Baby steps! Isabel would point to the words and read aloud, "Habia una vez (*Once upon a time* in Spanish)." Then she would hold the Teddy bear's paw, point to the words and repeat in her adorable, high-pitched Teddy bear voice, "Habia una vez."

Mystery Reader

To encourage attendance, Wednesdays became "Mystery Reader Day" in my class. The kids knew that on Wednesdays – at some point in the day – a mystery guest was going to come read to our class. Sometimes it was a friend of mine, and other times it was one of my students' parents or a member of the community. And if I couldn't find anyone to come, I'd ask two of my students to go arrest another teacher, and she would come to my classroom to read to my students while I went to her classroom to read to her students.

Musical Chairs Reading

This one's fun. Play musical chairs, but when the music stops, there is a poem on every seat for children to read. Don't start the music again until children read their poems.

Multiple Perspectives

I have found that teaching kids to look at events from different points of view is a great way to help them build empathy. Reading offers a treasure trove of perspectives. When I was a kid I used to watch The Rocky & Bullwinkle Show. They had a wonderful feature called Fractured Fairy Tales where they told fairy tales in a little different way than their traditional tellings. Now there is an entire genre of books about fairy tales, nursery rhymes and other commonly known stories from different points of view. Why not share traditional versions with children, as well as alternative versions?

There are literally hundreds of different versions of Cinderella, from funny versions to scary versions to feminist versions. Familiar with the story of the Three Little Pigs? One of my favorite alternative versions to share with students is Jon Scieszka's and Lane Smith's The True Story of the Three Little Pigs, as told by the misunderstood wolf. Or why not grab a copy of The Three Little Wolves and the Big Bad Pig? The brilliance of these books is that they offer children food for thought about why certain events may happen.

IDENTIFYING DIFFICULTIES IN READING COMPRE-HENSION

I'd like to present you with a reading exercise. Please read the passage below:

The Muntkees lived in Shakiri during the gop rantiki. They were chirky people with large rafworts. They enjoyed kwertzing and eating tadilkins. Tadilkins were their staple food. Muntkees drogged tadilkins right off the tree and shared them with their corvabiks.

Alright, get ready because now you are going to take the state's standardized reading test – which will determine your placement in school for the rest of your life! Please orally answer these seven questions, and grade yourself afterwards (ANSWERS BELOW):

1. Who is this paragraph about?
2. Where do these people live?
3. When?
4. What kind of people were they?
5. What do they enjoy doing?
6. What was their staple food?
7. Who did they share it with?

ANSWERS: (1) Muntkees; (2) Shakiri; (3) during the gop rantiki; (4) chirky; (5) kwertzing and eating tadilkins; (6) tadilkins; (7) their corvabiks.

How did you do on the quiz? My guess is that you probably scored 100 percent, or close to it. Congratulations! You just earned a perfect score on a reading comprehension exam. So does that mean you understand what any of those underlined words mean?

Here is the problem with today's education system, with its rigid guidelines and love affair with standardized testing: we have created a generation of test-ready imbeciles who know how to fill-in bubbles but do not necessarily understand how to think critically. I've observed so many educators that offer vanilla ice cream programs that – if they would just try some of the engaging activities we discuss in this book –could offer unforgettable sundaes that entice children to read often and read more. Too many of us look at the world from our own point of view, ignoring the fact that many of our students may be looking at the world in an entirely different way.

So what's my point? Let's arm ourselves with lots of weapons of mass instruction in our arsenals as teachers and parents. Let's have a variety of approaches to meet the needs of different students. And parents need to understand their importance in this process.

In my trainings with parents, I always advise them to "pay attention" and not ignore the elephant in the room. If you are a parent who has been reading to and with your child, you have had the opportunity to observe up close your child's strengths, as well as areas that may require improvement. While you have probably spoken with your child's teacher, you must remember that your child's teacher has a lot of students in her care. YOU are your child's best teacher. YOU are your child's most important teacher. And YOU are the one who knows best.

What have you observed in your child? Does your child hate reading because of a total lack of interest? Does your child lack skill? Or is there something else going on?

There was a printed advertisement in a magazine many years ago advertising an oil change center, and the filthy mechanic smiled at the camera with the caption, "You can pay a little now or a lot later." What the ad was trying to say is you can invest 20 bucks in an oil change every 3,000 miles or you can wait for the engine to blow up and face a whopping bill. When your engine blows up, it should not come as much as a surprise. People with bad engines are guilty of not paying attention.

What I am getting at is that if you believe your child might have a reading disability as opposed to just a reluctance or disinterest in reading, you should get reading help now. Let's nip it in the bud while we can. You have a right to have your child tested at his school. If you'd like another opinion, have your child tested at a reading center or tutoring facility. Try to find a place where the test results don't necessarily benefit whoever is doing the testing. As grateful as I am for many tutoring centers, some are less interested in helping students and more interested in getting your money.

You know your child better than anyone. Trust your gut. I've learned that when my wife has a gut feeling about something, we need to follow her instinct. Better safe than sorry. Don't wait if you think your child has a serious problem. Get your child tested so you can know for sure. If there is a problem, sticking your head in the sand won't make it go away. Don't worry about social appearances. I have a Ph.D. in education with an expertise in reading development, and I have had all three of my children tested for their language and literacy skills. Two of my children had developmental speech delays, but since we caught it early, we were able to get my children excellent tutoring services that allowed them to start kindergarten on par with their peers. In my state, such testing is actually paid for with taxes collected from tobacco sales – and these examinations are free, regardless of parental income!

I've seen many of my friends insist their children had no language or reading problems. So what happens? These children struggle in school, and it only gets tougher as they advance in grades. It's one thing providing extra services to a first grader who is a little behind in reading; it's quite a different challenge trying to help a seventh grader improve.

I'm not saying seventh graders are lost causes. I have personally helped middle schoolers and high school students dramatically improve in reading. But all those years struggling took a toll, and these students could have benefitted so much more if their parents had just sought help earlier.

So today, my challenge to you is this: speak with your child's teacher and see how your child has been progressing since you started implementing the tips offered in this book. Ask the teacher's opinion on your child's reading outlook, and if you think that your child's struggles may be bigger than just a lack of interest or skill, ask your child's school to test your child. Ask for referrals to local agencies that can test your child, and find out the costs. I know people that will spend days online comparing the prices of jeans, but they'll just go to the first center they see to get their child tested. Do your homework and find out the best fit for your child – if it's necessary. Remember, you can pay a little now or a lot later. Let's make sure your child is having the most positive school experience possible.

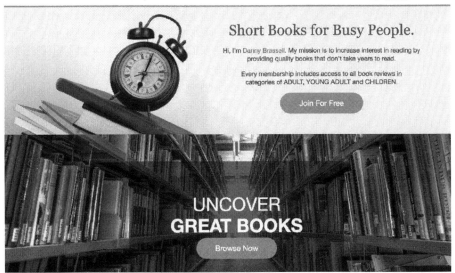

Interested in becoming a better reader, but you don't think you can find the time to read? Then you should join www.lazyreaders.com, where we provide short books for busy people. Every month you will receive 10 book recommendations: 3-4 adult-level, 3-4 young adult-level and 3-4 children's books all under 250 pages. Your subscription is FREE.

Motivate and Inspire Others!
"Share This Book" and
"Download The MP3s"

Secrets of Successful Readers

Engaging Comprehension Strategies for School and Home

Here's a book you'll read in an hour and remember for a lifetime! While many people understand the importance of reading, successful leaders make a point of reading a lot. Danny shares the research-based, classroom-tested strategies that successful readers utilize each day. Plus, you'll get tips on award-winning children's books that will inspire reluctant and struggling readers. –$29.97

And Treat Yourself to One of Danny's Highly Popular Presentations on MP3!

Comprehension That Works (60 mins) –$19.97

75+ Reading Strategies (75 mins) –$19.97

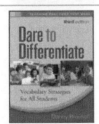

Dare to Differentiate: Vocabulary Strategies for All Students (75 mins) –$19.97

Working with English Language Learners (75 mins) –$19.97

…*and over 20 additional talks available.*

Special Quantity & Bundle Package Discounts Available!

Available on Amazon & at Select Education Events Near You!

Made in the USA
Columbia, SC
02 October 2018